The Wind in Both Ears

The WIND *in Both* EARS

Angus H. MacLean

UNITARIAN UNIVERSALIST ASSOCIATION
Boston
Revised edition published by arrangement with Beacon Press.
Second edition. Posthumously revised.

The author gratefully acknowledges permission to reprint passages from *W. H. Auden: Collected Poems* by W. H. Auden, edited by Edward Mendelson. Reprinted by permission of Random House, Inc. Copyright © 1945 by W. H. Auden. From *My Country, A Poem of America*, by Russell W. Davenport. Copyright © 1944, published by Simon and Schuster, Inc. From *The Poetry of Robert Frost* edited by Edward Connery Lathem. Copyright © 1969 by Holt, Rinehart and Winston, Inc. Copyright © 1962 by Robert Frost. Copyright © 1975 by Lesley Frost Ballantine. Reprinted by permission of Henry Holt and Company, Inc. From *The Thought and Art of Albert Camus* by Thomas Hanna. Copyright © 1959, published by Regnery Gateway Company. From *The Poems of Emily Dickinson*, edited by Thomas H. Johnson, Cambridge, Mass.: The Belknap Press of Harvard University Press, Copyright © 1951, 1955, 1979, 1983 by The President and Fellows of Harvard College. From *The Undiscovered Self* by C. J. Jung. Copyright © 1957, published by Little, Brown, and Company in association with the Atlantic Monthly Press. From *Modern Man in Search of A Soul* by C. J. Jung, published by Harcourt Brace Jovanovich, Inc. From *J. B.: A Play in Verse* by Archibald MacLeish. Copyright © 1956, 1957, 1958, by Archibald MacLeish. Copyright © renewed 1986 by William H. MacLeish and Mary H. Grimm. Reprinted by permission of Houghton Mifflin Company.

This reprint of The Wind in Both Ears *has been made possible through the generosity of the St. Lawrence Foundation for Theological Education.*

The Unitarian Universalist Association is committed to using gender-inclusive language in all of its publications. In this edition the text has been revised by mutual agreement of the author's children and the Association to conform to gender-inclusive usage. In the interest of historical authenticity, quoted matter is printed, as in the first edition, in its original form.

Library of Congress Cataloging-in-Publication Data

MacLean, Angus Hector, 1892-1969.
  The wind in both ears.

  Bibliography: p.
  1. Liberalism (Religion) 2. MacLean, Angus Hector, 1892-1969. 3. Unitarian Universalist Association--Clergy--Biography. I. Unitarian Universalist Association. II. Title.
BR1615.M27 1987   288   87-13763
ISBN 0-933840-30-6

To the people
of The First Unitarian Universalist Church,
Cleveland

Preface to the Revised Edition

The *Wind in Both Ears* was written in the early 1960s, and the language of the first edition reflects the universal use of male-dominant gender in reference to the collective singular in describing affairs human and godly, a trait of the English language before the early 1970s. Some postfeminist readers might find the repeated use of the words "man," "mankind," and "his" to be offensive when the meaning is not gender-specific.

When the Unitarian Universalist Association considered reprinting "The Wind in Both Ears," the editorial staff concluded that the book ought to be revised to meet current Unitarian Universalist Association objectives by removing gender-specific words where they seemed inappropriate. Because Angus Hector MacLean died in 1969, they asked us, his son and daughter, to approve of a revision.

We felt the wisdom of this request to be questionable. We remain most concerned about the ethics of changing the words written by an author who can no longer make these changes. We also worry about the artistic damage we may be doing to a well-written book and the subtle changes in meaning that may water down his message.

In spite of these concerns, we have reluctantly consented to the printing of the necessary changes. We hope that, in an effort to compromise to meet current perceptions, we have followed the premise of "The Message is the Method."[1]

COLIN DUART MACLEAN
SUSANNE MACLEAN BOONE

February, 1987

---

[1]Title of an address given by Angus H. MacLean at the centennial dinner of the Universalist Sabbath School Union. Published by the Universalist Church of America. Date not given.

Preface

In this book, Angus MacLean takes a long and honest look at himself and at his fellow religious liberals. But he knows that religious liberals are not confined to his own church, and he addresses them wherever they happen to be.

Dr. MacLean, a Unitarian Universalist minister, claims for his church that it has, to a greater degree than any other of comparable size, dropped the doctrinal burdens and attachments of the old world religions, and that it has demonstrated unity in diversity of belief on both national and local levels. But he sees his church's failures as well as its positive achievements, and he charges that although religious liberals have succeeded in discarding doctrines and creeds they have not rid themselves of the age-old tendency toward evil. They are by no means immune to the general temptation to evade, sidestep, and pervert the truth, and they are too often satisfied to give mere verbal devotion to the values they acclaim as theirs. He insists that they need discipline and devotion as much as any religious group ever did.

The author writes with real knowledge of the problems and conflicts of modern human beings, and of those with which the religious liberal and his church are particularly afflicted. He states them clearly, and deals with them honestly, humbly, and in full realization of the responsibility we all share to meet and solve them. But because he also writes as one who belongs in his universe and world, and feels at home in them, this book offers hope, encouragement, and confidence.

"I speak as a man at worship, and not as a prophet," Dr. MacLean writes. It is because we all possess enough virtues and vices to merit one another's respect and compassion that we expect so much from church.

Born in Nova Scotia in 1892, Angus MacLean received his early education in Canadian public schools. He says that, under Presbyterian auspices, traveling by horseback, he "preached the Gospel all over the Canadian plains" before he entered college. He was graduated from McGill University and from its Theological School. He taught at Columbia University Teachers' College for four years, and received his Ph.D. there. In 1928 he became Professor of Religious Education at the Theological School of St. Lawrence University, where he remained until 1960, serving as Dean from 1951 to 1960. Since then he has been Minister of Education at the First Unitarian Universalist Church, Shaker Heights, Ohio.

He has made an incalculable contribution to the educational program of the Unitarian Universalist denomination, both as teacher and inspirer of a long succession of classes of young ministers-to-be and as a consultant in the development of the impressive Beacon Curriculum for Religious Education. He now continues his contribution, working at the intimate personal level of the local church, preaching, and creating a program of parent education.

Dr. MacLean acknowledges a great indebtedness to the Presbyterian background of his boyhood and youth for its non-theological values, such as its appeal to integrity and its respect for scholarship. He is grateful to his Methodist teachers in theological school for giving a social dimension to his thinking, enabling him for the first time to see the individual in the context of society. It was this very upbringing and exposure, he believes, that made it impossible for him to become anything other than a religious liberal. He became a Unitarian Universalist, not as a rebel or a come-outer, but as one discovering congenial souls. As a Presbyterian he had assumed that one must fight for his soul. He found it easier, he says, to maintain his soul in Unitarian Universalism.

ROBERT KILLAM

THE FIRST UNITARIAN UNIVERSALIST CHURCH OF CLEVELAND
OCTOBER, 1964
REVISED FEBRUARY, 1987

Contents

The Wind in Both Ears

CHAPTER 1

The Purging of Religion

The progressive disenchantment with religion was a movement with a long history when I was born. There had been the Renaissance, the Protestant revolt, the Enlightenment, the Encyclopedists, and the Darwinian evolutionists and their less-than-Darwinian interpreters in the fields of religion, politics, and commerce. The gods had withstood a long siege when I came into the world, and maybe they withstood it because the common folks were still largely unaware of what was happening. At that time any young cleric with an ambition for scholarship or for ecclesiastical status spent some time in post-seminary study in German universities, and in this select company of postgraduates names such as Adolf von Harnack were on everyone's lips. Reason and science had assumed authority once regarded as the special preserve of God's appointees. An unprecedented scientific-historical analysis of the Christian scriptures and the Christian tradition followed the spread of the idea of Evolution in the second half of the nineteenth century. The Bible became a book, the Christ was reduced to human dimensions, and the very existence of the Jesus of history could be inferred but not proved. The authorship of statements traditionally attributed to Jesus was called in question at almost any point one could mention. Sacred writings long regarded as of divine origin became highly edited documents from a variety of sources. In the general literary field "this believing world" was featured as incredibly naive, and modern men and women readied themselves to step forth, free from all falsehood, to face a new world. At the same time revolutions toppled

1

thrones and monarchs and prelates, and so people also prepared themselves for a world freed from political tyranny. Out of it all came the positive developments of rationalism, individualism, socialism, and democracy. The retreating gods fought a rearguard action, and seemed destined to leave behind a heritage of mere literary symbolism for the new world.

And so it happens that today, when my generation has reached its threescore years and ten, I find myself associated with a religious fellowship that eagerly absorbed the new knowledge, the new scientific attitudes, the personal liberation, the naturalistic rationalism, and the humanistic tendencies of recent centuries. And this is a fellowship that is also progressively severing itself from its parent historic stream, going beyond it to adopt other historic traditions, too, and add them to its resources. It is a fellowship that faces the new world with largely unquestioned faith in the individual's potential, and is wishful of building a happy earthly home. This fellowship is now being overtaken, not by newer movements so much as by life's realities, and this is one of the facts with which this book is concerned.

How completely we were caught up in the push of history! And how necessary and rewarding the experience of personal liberation from the old orientations! How inescapable it all was for so many of us! It may seem not too flattering to suspect that we were as much a product of our time and history as the monastic movement was of its time. This, however, does not rob us of the genuineness of our liberation. This time of ours, however, has seen bridges burned behind advancing humanity that were never burned before. It has put powers into the hands of the individual he or she never had before, and the individual has achieved a new sense of being. But as some forgotten realities of life again begin to close in upon one, there's a difference.

We reflect certain elements in the philosophies of the last three or four centuries as well as the more ancient cultures. We reflect the spirit of the Enlightenment and of the scientific movement as it affected scholarship and commerce. In us, too, are the classic protests in behalf of the common individual, or rather of humanity as such, and of the dreams of one's emancipation and happiness, voiced by so many—Beatrice and Sidney Webb, Karl Marx, Walter Rauschenbusch, Eugene Debs and other labor leaders, the Wobblies, as the members of the I.W.W. were called, and that sweet-spirited Jesus whom we conjured out of the disenchanted gospel records and who lived with us and served us so well for a short time. We think

2

in the tradition of Charles S. Peirce, William James, John Dewey and their kindred spirits of the arts and social sciences. Yet individually we are not like any of them, for the individual varies within any given system, and in our convictions transcends them all as a primary object of value. We are in a vital tradition, broader than any specific religious tradition, drawing from "secular" wisdom and from the traditions of other faiths for our own religious use. This faith has a history-making potential, provided it can make some headway against weaknesses to which humans, as such, are born heirs, and so does not succumb to the resurgent and revitalized evil that came on the heels of liberation, feeding on our oversights, our errors, and our simplicity.

The tragedy of our era is the discovery that on the verge of a great human triumph, when the tools and resources we thought would make for human happiness are in human hands, the world can still put on an unparalleled exhibition of bestiality and tyranny; that in the midst of the triumph of reason, reason itself can be rationally repudiated and indeed enslaved to serve irrational ends; that democracy can be found wanting by many of the insurgent peoples on the move out of age-old want and tyranny; that personal liberty as the basic social value can be repudiated and be seriously threatened in freedom's great political strongholds. Evils once sponsored by the old gods and kings have had no difficulty in finding new sponsors. Reason, human compassion, democracy, and the self-ruled individual are embattled and re-engaged by the old enemies; the American dream fades and the hope of the world is enfeebled.

And so, as might have been expected, some great minds and spirits now call the world to account again in the name of the supernatural powers, and the old categories of wisdom have a new lease on life. Europe has produced ably represented theologies and philosophies of despair. Reason, the beloved whom we trusted and in whom our souls delighted, can and often does find life meaningless and absurd and so discredits itself; can and often does find morality to be so much nonsense, and nature itself can be found to be basically defective. The brilliant and appealing Albert Camus goes beyond absurdity, but cannot find any better way to save his sense of being than to declare eternal enmity to "God." Mother nature, admittedly beautiful and wonderful, is freakish, ruthlessly indifferent to the human plight, and as intellectually impenetrable as the old gods. Others, among whom many of us are numbered, stubbornly cling to a humanism that is but poorly supported by science, history, or theology.

A good deal of what I have reviewed was still in the future when Kierkegaard found life to be absurd, and in his leap of faith, as Camus suggests, abandoned the struggle to make sense of it. In our time minds of great endowment have followed him in his appraisal of life, both theological and "secular" thinkers. There are thinkers among us too who, though purged of all religion and devoted to reason, still find that life is senseless, who do not sense any great tragedy in it all but find, more after the manner of a Mehetabel, that "life is too funny to explain." And in this feeling many lapse away from the pursuit of truth without any impulse toward a leap of faith.

Here in America our liberal fellowship has been protected from the terror Europe has had to face, and thus few indeed among us tend to repudiate the assumptions that life makes sense and is good. Nevertheless, we cannot any longer complacently accept some of our basic assumptions. While we make much of the right to think, there is nothing we need more than some thinking to undergird the faith we profess. It is still lightly assumed that if we set individuals free they will rise to their fine human potential, that if we let them think for themselves they will think wholesomely, that if we let them seek the truth for themselves they will really seek it, that if we let them manage their own lives and see that they are fed and clothed, and so forth, they will be good. In such assumptions there may lurk the ghost of future shock and disillusionment.

The image of God (or reality) that is left us is not too reassuring. God is a permissible concept, to be used or not. No philosophical or scientific concept representative of the reality that God once stood for has replaced it. God, as some existentialists use the term, has not been imported as yet, except as intellectual curiosity or a literary and poetic concept for the few. We are without any significant cosmic symbol.

But we are free, confident, openly declared for truth, whatever it may be, and at whatsoever price it may come, and this in the most general terms. We anticipate human unity, we worship something vague we call reality, we worship nature, and we venerate human personality as a primary value. We profess to seek to enlist all in a cooperative venture of rebuilding society, and to give the individual a chance to live on this earth securely, creatively, and happily. And more and more people are joining us daily to begin the round from hurt to protest, to cooperative fellowship in living and learning. We share a great ethical tradition with the Christian groups from which we emerged and from which we have been cut off, and we are more and more aware daily of what we share in value

4

experience with all the great world religions. But no church of comparable size and of such representative character sharing in this wide heritage is so happily disencumbered of the doctrinal burdens and attachments of the traditional religions. Here, at least, is an incalculable advantage.

The degree of freedom in religion that our group has attained in its corporate existence is no mean achievement. To my knowledge the like of it has never happened before. It has here and there demonstrated unity in diversity of belief on both the national and the local levels. It invites the hurt and the coerced to come and find their own salvation in fellowship with other seekers. And they come fast enough to endanger the genius of the free tradition before they can be matured in the faith. The surface evidence seems to be overwhelmingly favorable.

But there is within the fellowship that which should be of major concern to us—some feeling that all is not well, some apprehension. There is a wistful feeling, very common, that something most precious was left behind in the old faiths. There is the often spoken suspicion that liberals are less secure than the folks in credal churches. Some are chilled by what they call "intellectualism," and seem to believe that warmth of fellowship goes with orthodoxy. And there is a suspicion that we as a people do not wish to seek or abide by the truth as it affects human relations. More and more of our ministers express the fear that suburban classcism and privilege outdo the faith when and where the chips are down. Unitarian Universalists, as well as others, can watch serenely from the sidelines, uninvolved, while others are deprived of their liberties—and some of our members approve the deprivation. If truth supports these feelings, it is probably because we have been so unaware of the radically daring nature of our religious claims, and because we have been so unaware of the hazards these commendable claims created for us. To so dare without more disciplined group address to the world we live in is to invite eventual disaster.

These apprehensions of mine do not come from any nostalgia for the old ways. How thankful I have been and am for the freedom and generosity of spirit, and the ethical vision permitted among us! I am apprehensive because I so love what we have found and dared, and because our faith has never been put to any severe test, protected as we are in a well-fed class in a warless continent. I speak not in judgment of others, for I am as deeply involved in the weaknesses of our faith as anyone. I speak as a man at worship, not as a prophet.

5

CHAPTER 2

The Truth's Surprise

Can a person look into the face of God and still live? We have assumed that one has the fortitude to withstand anything which searching for truth or human circumstance may reveal. Are we a people of unusual toughness of fiber, or are we, maybe, more wishful than wise? Are our anticipations with respect to the realities to be disclosed acute enough to deserve such confidence? I have often wondered how people of such minds as are posessed by T. S. Eliot, Carl Jung and others that could be named, should make so much of the supernatural. Have we confronted the realities that have made the supernatural necessary to them? And, going to the other extreme, have we looked through the eyes of a Jean Paul Sartre and seen what he has seen? What have we done with the realities that have produced a Heidegger and a Camus? A Kierkegaard and a Barth? Can such responses be without cause? Or can we, perhaps, be selective of the realities we take note of? Or can we be ambivalent, openly and deliberately, in our response to the universe? Or will the verdict of history be that a curse awaits those who try to sustain their spirits on the fruit of the tree of knowledge?

Possibly liberal religionists need not be frightened by visions that have driven others to despair, but they cannot afford to be indifferent to them, for they have yet to have the confrontation with the angel of God that shall bless or destroy them. There is reason to suspect that, in part at least, we have taken our material security, our good food and general immunity from want and danger, for courage and toughness and spiritual hardihood. We, at any rate, have not proved that our faith can survive the blazing, searing truths that have so profoundly disturbed so many, and conditioned the thinking of so many more.

It seems encouraging to know, however, that when the absurdities and horrors and contradictions of life have done their worst, one can still find some means of fulfillment, even when one believes in nothing beyond immediate experience. It is interesting to know that one's sense of being and of responsibility can even be enhanced under the worst circumstances. When all else fails, one can maintain one's souls by picking a quarrel with what one regards as a senseless universe, which means that one still has oneself. The individual is gifted with sources of strength and meaning that one cannot be aware of until put to the test. But when a person is reduced to thinking of life as nonsense, can such adjustment be more than the stand of a few courageous hearts, trapped in a universe that outrages their sensibilities? I don't know, but I suspect that such sterility of meaning means death to the many and maybe, eventually, to the few. And what about those who take the leap of faith out of absurdity and relay their hopes to the supernatural, of which some of them at least admit they know nothing at all? To leap in the dark, they feel, is better than the quest of evidential truth that never comes.

Shall we ever face the realities that such people have faced? If and when we do, what shall our response be? Shall we, too, abandon the effort? Actually we haven't even tried until very recently to make sense of life, although the responsibility to try was ours as soon as the old God failed us. Shall we find that we can withstand a face-to-face confrontation with the inconsistencies of the realities we experience, and of human bestiality, and still keep the faith? Or shall we find that "truth" does not come in the raw, that it has to be screened? Thirty years ago I should have regarded as nonsense the sentiments in these words by Emily Dickinson:

> Tell all the truth but tell it slant—
> Success in Circuit lies
> Too bright for our infirm Delight
> And Truth's superb surprise
> As lightning to the Children eased
> With explanation kind
> the Truth must dazzle gradually
> Or every man be blind—[1]

I find the statement arresting today. There is no implied suggestion in the use of this verse that we ever should, or could, deliberately temper the winds for the shorn lambs. I am concerned with winds that affect the shepherds as they do the sheep. Their fortitude is as much questioned as the lamb's. There is a strong possibility that one has the screening devices unconsciously within oneself, and that one may be prone to dodge some truths even when most free and most courageous. I suspect that while we have been busy condemning irrationality, and quite properly too, we have also been busy putting forth new coverings, as surely as the wild creatures put fourth fur and feathers to match the seasons. If the answer to the question implicit here is "yes," or even a "yes and no," that answer has to have a central place in our theologizing, our worship, and in our corporate deliberations.

Most of my life I have worshipped, as have so many others, the kindly, appealing presence that Wordsworth's heart went out to, choosing to ignore, for the moment at least, the meaning of the striking hawk, of the lightning that kills a child we love and cherish, of the millions of the blighted, unfulfilled lives of innocents. I, at least, must confess that while in the act of experiencing "the joy of elevated thought" the sparrow falls backstage in my mind. But more of that fall later.

The individual can get into an impersonal, objective mood, and observe bits of dark reality dispassionately. But it is far from permissible to conclude from this that one as a being can face reality in an inclusive and personal encounter and be equally unbiased. Secure in health, wealth, and status, one may think one has achieved this ability when it isn't really so. If the individual can look at all the realities unmoved, although personally involved as living beings, one is a beast or a vegetable. To absorb the inconsistencies and ruthlessness and indifference of nature in the large in one's own being, without any outreach beyond the realities, is to be less than human. As a youth I often shook my fist at the sky, which was supposed to be the residence of my Presbyterian God, and I protested and accused. I was sure that I had blasphemed at such times, but now, looking back, I feel these were among my most religious moments. But what does this notion of religiousness do to God? I find myself very close to Camus at this point, but I cannot rest where he does, or I should say, where I think he rests. We need to go beyond revolt as he went beyond absurdity. God, in what I can gather of his sense of the word, is the great ordaining, sustaining power of the universe, a power without sense or order available to man. But there is in my experience also a far-from-omnipotent God, the emergent sense of being that calls for order, and for sense and meaning and justice. I have often thought of God as the conscience of the universe. The sparrow falls and this God notes, in me at least. But, unlike Mark Twain, I find the fact that God just *notes* meaningful. That God can do nothing immediately about it is not so significant as that God notes it and makes a judgment upon it. This reality that I sense, my own being calling as it does for order and meaning, is also of the universe. In me I know the material of the universe breathes and thinks and values and wonders about itself, and prays and sings, and, what is more, demands, requires and hopes, even where nothing at all responds. There is here something of the utmost cosmic significance that the keepers of despair take too little to heart. I experience the universe as being in conflict as I am, and I take sides. I also stand in reverence before the persistence of life. This is to me the great confrontation and not death and mortality. The wasteful and prodigal methods governing life continuity suggest the strength of life's thrust. The thousands of germinating seeds from the tree or the salmon that never reach maturity ensure the continuity of these species. But we are shocked when we find this law operative in human society. Here at least, in the human, there may be hope of a process of elimination of wastefulness. We are significantly shockable, and there is good reason for faith in man's capacity to make it unnecessary, through control of birth and the sharing of necessities, for millions of babies to be born only to die soon after. Humanity has reached the point at which it may begin to take charge of its own evolution, and this has cosmic meaning. And isn't it also interesting to note that some creatures have but one young or one egg per season? Is there something more attuned to our sensitivies being worked out? Some things are for us "in the nature of things," else we should not be as we are. Summing up I would say that the universe is contradictory, but that its movements and direction are not senseless.

I like to observe how human efforts to use and despoil other humans hit back in the long run. The West is reaping the fruits of what it did in China and Africa for so many decades. The exploited seek the status and power and freedom of the exploiters. So much has happened in spite of the most powerful efforts to keep it from happening. Can the universe be really indifferent? While we set forth to segregate black from white, and to hold the black in subject status, the mingling of bloods goes on apace, indeed in direct relationship to the efforts put forth to "keep white pigment pure." There's an old Hebrew saying: "Man thinks; God laughs."

Moreover, the fact that one has a nature, that one has needs that sooner or later have to be respected, that make demands of the social order, is to me evidence that the universe is not always indifferent. The conflict within me, too, between my constructive and destructive impulses, is indicative of the incompatibility of many things that are, and of the fact of a struggle for emergence of more effective responses. So there is for me as "God" with whom I feel identified, and there is also the God to whom I respond ambivalently, and with whom I keep up certain quarrels.

But in this very insecure and unsatisfactory adjustment of mine, what screening and diluting of reality have gone on will be more easily observed by others than by me. And it is equally so with anyone who may read my writing, whether or not he or she loves or hates life, or finds it harmonious or nonsensical.

And now to the one fact that I feel all liberated souls must take to heart as they do few facts. We have rightly discarded many superstitions, many doctrines that we found wanting, many myths and many authorities, but we have not left behind one single human weakness or tendency, including many devices for evading reality— absorption and preoccupation with work or business, the use of entertainment and intoxicating beverages for our leisure hours, the liturgical veneration of values that are really avoided and neglected. In the latter category we can include the thinking of love while avoiding its practice, the veneration of thought by many who do not think, the identification of virtue with propriety and the respect of people of recognized status, the romantic illusion of superiority to the rest of humanity, the acceptance of the status quo as the sacred cow in our economic and political pastures. Who would dare say that we have abandoned such practices along with the traditional creeds? It is quite possible that we haven't any more courage in confronting the realities than had our forebears, and that we have to admit the existence of new dodges which accomplish the old end of evasion.

But what of the question asked at the beginning? Can a person look into the face of God and retain hope and avoid despair? I think that maybe one can without betraying either one's mind or heart. And probably Kierkegaard never took a longer leap than I take in saying that. I think some people have demonstrated this ability rather wonderfully. But if we assume that this is done by casual notioning and surmising in an uninvolved way while so many others are at

11

grips with death and all its allies, we assume a great deal. If we assume further that successful confrontation is the work of reason alone, we assume too much. Reason can give over to despair before the heart does. By which, let me hasten to say, I mean that an individual can will to live when there seems to be no rational justification for living.

CHAPTER 3
Religion Is Many Things

A mong the problems the inquirer finds in the task of thinking out his or her faith, not the least is that of understanding what religion is. The common notion that religion can be defined in a brief, definite statement has occasioned a lot of the difficulty. Religion is a variety of things, and this is apparent in both its contradictory personal moods and in its historic manifestations. Nevertheless, although so varied, there has been a kind of unity about it. Among the great religions, at least, there is a common core of ethical values. All religions address themselves to the same basic, human problems. And the prevalence of prayer and liturgy and moral codes in most formal religions indicate that they have much in common in the manner of expression. The differences, however, are very real, and disconcerting enough to make the verbal representation of religion exceedingly difficult. It cannot be done at all briefly, although even the best scholars seem to be under some compulsion to make the attempt.

Definitions of religion range from the wholly natural to the wholly supernatural; from religion as ethical concern to something to which the ethical is irrelevant, or at best, secondary. The late Professor E. S. Ames, of the University of Chicago, defines religion in purely social-ethical terms, as do John Dewey and many others. Alfred North Whitehead says many, many wise things about it, including the popular statement that religion is what a man does with his solitariness, and it is wise to remember that that is not all he said about religion. Sociologists are inclined to think of religion in terms of institutional patterns and loyalties. Many think of it in terms of personal and mystical inwardness. So it can hardly be contained in any one definition, as every good descriptive account, such as William James' "Varieties," indicates.[1] Varieties are apparent even within any one fellowship, and probably the needs of individual souls are responsible. An individual's religion can be a complex of diverse moods and feelings and convictions.

A Chinese author of a best seller of some years ago said that in the old orient one could belong to several quite different faiths at the same time without seeming to be a victim of indecision or of inconsistency: one worships in the religious pattern one's mood-of-the-occasion suggests, which seems to me rather sensible. Aren't there times when one feels like an Episcopalian or a Methodist or a Presbyterian? To be a Unitarian Universalist all the time is almost too much to ask of one. While I consider myself a strong nonconformist I could, at times, be a liturgist, enjoying the symbols, sounds, and rhythms of familiar and classical-historical expressions of prayer and praise. There are times when I have a strong sense of historic continuity. When the demands of the mind are uppermost, I crave stark realism. There are times when I tend to follow the prophets of righteousness, seeking to put right a world that has gone out of joint. There are times when my religious feelings are focused in a sense of, and concern for, my personal integrity; when what I am at heart seems more important to maintain than life itself. There are times when I care not at all for realism or formalism or even for the clamor for righteousness, and I become primarily a mystic. There are times when I despair of reason and times when I find in it the very voice of God. I can also be a dancing, singing, joyous celebrant of the good things of life, for religion is also festive. And I doubt if any one mood is more or less religious than any other.

We can think of people, too, whose religions are as different from each other as herrings are from hot dogs but who, nevertheless, are all deeply religious. I think of Joe Martin, who works in a bank but should have been a theologian. He reads seriously and effectively in philosophy and theology. A seeking to find intellectual light amid life's mysteries characterizes him—otherwise he is not remarkable. Is Martin religious? We should have to be tightly confined in mind to say he is not.

Take one of the great theologians: Soren Kierkegaard, for instance, of whom I once heard another theologian complain that he never in his life lifted a finger to help anyone or tried to affect society or reduce human ills. This judgment, although perhaps excusable from the perspective of a socially concerned person of the 1920's, is nevertheless hardly fair. Kierkegaard had his own kind of moral fortitude and to a classical degree. He thought, and with such consequence that theologians and psychiatrists today avidly study his works for light on the ills of the human spirit. A man of prodigious mind, but an odd-ball who dealt ruthlessly with "Christians" and sinners alike, and sought for the truth beyond the reach of reason, and found it through some faculty other than reason. How different from St. Francis of Assisi or Billy Sunday, and yet how religious!

There is a primary emphasis among us on truth-seeking. No one expects us to come forth with *the* truth humanity needs, but we often do find sustaining truths for ourselves, even though they be no more than happy organizations of feelings. And this is religious. I have often quoted the Indian Tagore as saying that to seek the truth is to admit its separateness, and that a greater endeavor is to *be* the truth, and this without doubt is high religion. Sophia Fahs quotes a child's definition of God: "God is what knows how to grow." I think Tagore would agree.

This *being* the truth appears in many variations even within our culture. There's Mrs. Sims, for many years a parishioner of mine. She did not know what to make of life. She said it puzzled her, which many of us would consider an understatement today. She didn't think seeking the truth was very rewarding. She rather found release and a sense of worth through her generosity towards people and creatures. Tramps, stray dogs and cats, the sick, the worried, and the bereaved always seemed to find their way to her door. She took the command to "judge not" literally. "I find the judging of people too difficult," she said, "so I treat them all alike." "What people deserve doesn't concern me." When her neighbors remonstrated with her for trusting people too much, after her house had been entered and robbed, she replied, "I've been robbed legally and politely all my life, so why should the illegal appropriation of my meagre property be so different?" And what a company this woman has among those "who seek to lessen the world's pain and relieve its miseries" in some small way! These are the people who find it easier to represent their religion in an operational pattern rather than in a theological system.

I could also give the names of people who are mystically inclined, and even within this category there is quite a variety. An old minister friend of mine was called a "solitary." He should not have been a minister, for he had very few social assets. He was quiet, lonely, and inward looking—a churchy kind of mystic—the kind who is likely to see visions that are quite peculiar to his denomination, even though received as from God. His counterparts are among the great mystics, Protestant and Catholic.

There are also the nonconformist mystics, who disregard all approaches but their own feelings and insights. There are the nature mystics too, often found among Universalists and Unitarians, whose theological horizons may be indefinite but whose sense of being and kinship envelop the universe. There are mystics such as Gandhi who are quite ethically minded and are involved in furthering the good in human society. Some feel that they transcend ethics, even to the point where ethical concern seems irrelevant and is at best but a natural byproduct of godliness. Perhaps Evelyn Underhill is as near as any to this category.

And there is the human being of social passion who expresses his or her faith in connection with the larger social problems; intellects of such unexcelled passion as Walter Rauschenbusch of the 1920's. We find others with similar fervor, who have no connection with churches and profess no significant ideology, but who can labor— and even die—for the human cause, without pride, protest, or fanfare.

And religion finds its expression in gloom, unhappiness, and fear. Folks in my home parish used to regard as a sign of godliness the fact that their minister had never been known to smile. It occurred to us kids that he might just be a common sourpuss, but no adult suspected this truth. In the same church was an elder whose religious expressions were a tearful bewailing of the sins of humanity and fear for their souls and his own. And was he religious!

There have been times in the lives of people—and great people too—when they passed through what some speak of as "fear and trembling" and "the sickness unto death," when life seemed to lose its meaning. Tolstoy, for instance. At a time when he should have been completely happy, judging from his circumstances, life lost all meaning and value, and he wished to be rid of it. He had a rope and he would hide it at night for fear he might rise and hang himself. He would not accept invitations from his friends to go hunting, for fear of the impulse to shoot himself. He said, "I did not know what I wanted, I was afraid of life; and I was driven to leave it, and in spite of that I still hoped for something from it."[2] Yet this was a creative despair, although it might very well have been "sickness of soul," as William James calls it.

16

Kierkegaard found his wisdom beyond the despair of the mind, which could only confront him with the mystifying, the illogical, contradictions, paradoxes, and absurdities. And the way he resolved the paradoxes and absurdities was to see them as the manward side of the truth—that was whole only in the eye of God—and the agent of this achievement was faith. Such historic facts make me hopeful that someone may in our time make sense of the monumental absurdities of man's divinity and animality with which we contend.

Even in our ordinary lives, we find something of the sombre quality that is the mark of real religion. Facing stern and unpleasant realities is both religious and disturbing. Seeing oneself as one is can be a very unhappy religious illumination. Seeing the world as it is today is the most appalling of all experiences for modern people and religion intensifies the anguish the situation stirs in us. I am sure that many souls are today driven to the verge of despair, if not over the edge, and if we survive the immediate future, we shall hear from them in one way or another. This despair may lead to constructive or destructive enterprises. Great dedication, great scholarship, and high art may come from it, and so may also the destroyers of whom we have had more than enough already.

The classics of religion also show, in the phenomenon of religious ecstasy, an extreme opposite to this despair, which is perhaps paralleled in a small way in the lives of ordinary healthy people. So we might go on citing varieties of moods and experiences associated with religion. We might be a bit more daring and ask if people like the killers of John Huss and Servetus and their kind were religious? If, perhaps, Hitler was religious? Or, if the Soviet Union is laboring under a kind of religious compulsiveness? My answer to all of these would be in the affirmative. There is evidence, insofar as the U.S.S.R. is concerned, that even products of that culture, i.e., those still behind the Iron Curtain, regard Sovietism as a religion.

And all this brings forth one point, namely, that religion may be inescapable, but it is not necessarily good. To recognize this, or to look at it this way, will solve a lot of problems. We don't have to decide, for instance, who is or is not religious. To say that religion is always good, but that we rarely ever have it, leaves us without knowing what or where it is, or if it will ever be. To say, as some preachers do, that religion has never been tried is nonsense. If religion had always been good, considering its universal manifestation in all historic times and places, we should not be faced with such a world as confronts us now.

It is in the face of great crises that religions have been most creative, and at times equally faulty. When religion undertakes to build and restore, it is often magnificent. I often think of what happened in England immediately after the John Wesley revival. The public life of England had been as low as that of France or any other country, if not worse. But count the great figures who rebuilt England, making revolution such as happened in France unnecessary, and building honor, high responsibility, dignity, and integrity into public offices and services. Then count among these the followers of Wesley, and one may get some sense of the creative power of religion. On the other hand, when religion gets wedded to the status quo or commands society in complacency, it degenerates. When it begins to eliminate oppositon and purge theological deviants, nothing can do more harm. The Spanish inquisition, the persecution of the Scottish Covenanters and the like are shameful and guilt-producing chapters of history. There have also been times when young religions have spawned like insects and spread destruction to all who would not yield to them—the Islamic conquests, for example.

Religion is inescapable except for those who can live as superficially as animals. Then, out of the necessity of religion, comes the question, "How do I know that religion is ever any good? How know that it is doing good rather than harm?" One advantage the great institutional religions had was that somewhere within their traditions or sacred books they had correctives that reformers could pick up and use for the restoration or purification of the faith. I wish that our industrial system had such built-in integral correctives. One of the first reads as follows, "And what does the Lord require of thee, but to do justly, to love mercy, and to walk humbly with your God." To live justly, be of good will, and walk humbly before life's mysteries and necessities, and before the gulf that separates us from the ideals we profess. One inspired by such values has capacity for growth and self-judgment. We are indebted to modern thinkers for other yardsticks, some of which are the same as Hosea's. From the psychoanalysts come these: To live love, to cultivate the art of giving and receiving love, to exercise one's religion in complete freedom—for if it isn't free it is not likely one's own—to seek to lessen the world's pain, etc.

Gordon Allport, the psychologist, says of the mature religious sentiment that

1. It is well differentiated. It is individual uniqueness.
2. It is dynamic in character despite its derivative nature.
3. It is productive of a consistent morality.

4. It is comprehensive—embraces all life.
5. It is integral.
6. It is fundamentally heuristic—investigative, truth seeking.[3]

These are also the ways by which we judge the maturity of a person, ways by which we differentiate between the worthy and unworthy in religion. We can add other checks: Religion requires integrity. Religion does not serve us best insofar as it seeks to have a corner on the truth and to confine us within its statements of truth. When it so fails in humility it is diseased. Religion is limited and blighted insofar as its value or moral obligations apply only to one people or class of people. Religion is a disservice to us when it becomes irrelevant to the issues of life, or when it outrages human nature in any way, or when it thwarts unavoidable natural functioning and condemns it as evil. When such thwartings are not a disservice to humanity as might be the case with the Shakers and the medieval Cathari, they do violence to themselves, and actually have removed themselves from existence.

There are plenty of yardsticks. The honest appraisal of religion is possible, and is contingent upon the desire and will for it.

Were I a complacent liberal I should now exclaim that these very yardsticks indicate that the good kind of religion is the one we liberals profess to practice. The human tendency to assume that *we* are the chosen and favored of God is a constant and universal threat. The religion we profess may stand up very well as a profession of faith, but my personal religion, known to me especially well, is where I need to go to work with my yardsticks. Are what we do and think relevant to the crises of our time? Do we sense any kind of lesson for us in the biblical figure who smote his chest and prayed with such directness and simplicity, "God be merciful to me a sinner"? Does our religion have a command in it that we cannot evade? Does it lead to the sticking out of necks now and then, or is it always the guardian of our undisturbed feelings?

When I began writing these paragraphs, my mind was practically immobilized by preoccupation with the atomic war threat. I have been so anguished over it that it seems to me that anything I could say would be irrelevant, for this terror has put a shadow of tragedy on all things, from the laughter of children, to great political and social enterprises, to the wisdom of the wisest, and even to the song of birds. What's the use of anything if we, or most of us, are to be obliterated tomorrow? I know this will be judged as a "sick" feeling, but I confess to it, for it has affected me deeply. If only a few of us could die to save us all! But even that might be futile. I mentioned this frustrated feeling to a friend, and he said something that helped: "If catastrophe comes it won't matter what we say now, but if we can hold off disaster, what we say now can matter a great deal." And it's even more true of what we do.

As a member of our Western culture, I feel guilt and shame for what we failed to do throughout the years of our great opportunity. I would ask for mercy for our current self-righteousness that finds no fault in ourselves, and all the faults in the enemy—for this failure to take our full share of the blame for what has happened to the world, I'd ask for mercy, if I knew where to ask. But I don't know where because I cannot credit any deity that is not demoniac with what we face. I grieve over the fact that our values, so beautifully conceived in universal terms, must still be merely tribal in a day when travel and commerce have crowded us all into one house of life.

So the questions for us now are: Can we appraise ourselves in the face of such a crisis as confronts us now? Or is this a time for shortsightedness, for bigotry and violence, and the abdication of all the values by which we claim to have lived? I can only answer that the greatest appraisals have come out of crises involving the shocking confrontation of the realities. Whether we can outface, outsmart, or outfight the external enemy is a secondary matter. The real enemy is war, and the great temptation and threat is to succumb to it. It is my hope that religion can still awaken us to this kind of realism.

In a review of the works of the Yugoslav Ivo Andric, Nobel prize winner, the reviewer speaks of 1961 as "Doomsday Eve." He says that on Doomsday Eve the world showed its gratitude to the person whose life and work expressed such a vision of human hope by giving appropriate praise and a purse of money, and then he adds, "the world went home and prepared for the slaughter." I never knew such pessimism and it has infected so much of writing and public utterance! I find it on my own tongue as though it didn't really come from me. Yet in a time that produces such pessimism, this man who was honored could speak of intelligence as something significant, could speak for the instinctive worth of every individual that can fashion a world that is not wholly terrifying and absurd, can still speak for effort as meaningful, and of hope as not always and everywhere vain. Surely our faith can speak no less for us.

Once, during a Christmas vacation, I visited a classroom in the school I served, and found four mice in a wastebasket. Something distracted me so that I did not release them. A week later I came again to the unused room and found one lively mouse in the basket and three tails. It was because of this experience that mice talk from my wastebasket in my hearing as I write now. One just said, "Let's face it. We'll never get out of here unless someone lets us out, which is unlikely. And," he concluded, "the history of mice confined as we are is that they fight it out and the victors eat the vanquished until only one is left. So I guess that all but one of us are for it."

And then another fellow stuttered as he stretched to twice his usual height, "But, but, but, why can't we change this history of ours?" And both of these "meeces" could be called religious. I prefer the religion of the hopeful, active one.

Just so! Whatever we forget in these times, let us not forget (and this is the most hopeful thing I can say) that it is in times of supreme crisis that people become gods and human societies become redemptive.

21

CHAPTER 4

Religion and the Intellect

Religion and the intellect have not been at ease with each other throughout history. This very statement contains a falsehood that has contributed to the tension between the two, and that falsehood is the assumption that the intellect is not itself involved in religion. In dealing with religion we are concerned with the individual's powers, drives, needs, and capacities, including reasoning capacity. Should we not perhaps regard the historic tension as being between facets of experience? Between human need and the logic of a situation, or between the beloved adjustment one has made and the fresh inroads of new experience? Reason is involved in defense of the old as well as in the promotion of new insight. It is also true that the urgencies of the human heart have been known to defy the logic of both theology and settled customs in the interest of human good. I am far from being clearheaded about all this, but of this much I am sure: we need to understand better the intellectual dimension of religion, and something of the role of emotion in the functioning of the intellect.

There never was a time when the world's people needed the guidance of high intelligence as they do in our time, never a time when religions, both sacred and secular, so needed it. There never was time when people so needed dedication to commonly shared and historically tested values as they do now. The tragedy of the world is that earnest hearts are so often aflame in the promotion of violence as a solution to the world's problems, and equally true that so many of the world's greatest intellects give themselves with sacrificial devotion to the support of causes quite in opposition to the great and common needs of mankind. Today as never before, superior minds are cultivated and conserved and set to work as factional power assets. Historically, reason has been a troublemaker and a breaker-up of systems, thus serving a creative purpose. Now we know that it can be just power put to almost any use. Both human emotion and the human intellect can be used as power, while human needs go begging. Some say that if the powers and disciplines of human emotion and intellect can be wedded together in the interest of the human cause, the world is not yet without its hope, nor without the stuff of great dreams that make great souls and create cultures to match social crises as they arise. But a word of caution here. We used to discuss, and occasionally still do, the conflict between science and religion. We need to be reminded that religion and science have gotten together in more than one political upheaval which has recently threatened the world. The issue is not that they just get together, but that that togetherness serve man as such. Join they must. Apart from each other one is blind and the other impotent to do what needs to be done. But while we discuss this getting together, let us *not* forget that this is not the end of the matter. The question of the ends served remains.

Throughout history, religion has shown an ambivalent regard for the intellect. In many of the oldest religions we find crude superstitions and practices culturally bound with the sublimest insights into the realities of human experience. We find this ambivalence in Christian history, too. Christian leaders made excellent use of the mind while at the same time fearing it and vigorously countering its free operation. The search for and the use made of biblical manuscripts in order to establish the authenticity or falsity of records is one of the great achievements of the human intellect. It is worth noting also that the great theologians were intellectuals who mastered to an enviable degree the learning of their names. Origin and Aquinas are not equalled often in history, but as types they were not exceptions. They were, in their dedication to learning, typical of the great theological tradition. Sometimes clerics such as Copernicus and Mendel are so identified with their scientific work that few remember that they were clerics. Even today Albert Schweitzer is not the only one working in Africa and elsewhere who has mastered both theology and medicine. I remember that in the great university in which I did my undergraduate work a majority of the faculty were either clergy,

24

ex-clergymen, or the sons of clergymen. I need hardly mention the degree to which the great institutions of learning in this country and elsewhere were initiated and nurtured by religion, nor that religion has still a most respected place in them. The motivation was different in the old days, as knowledge was different. When a misplaced iota subscript in a Greek manuscript or unceretainty about Hebrew vowels meant that one's soul's salvation was at stake, or when learning was necessary as a means of outwitting the Devil, scholarship was assured. Such motivation is gone today, but biblical research and reasoning go on unabated. Many religious leaders wait eagerly for the pronouncements of nuclear physicists, psychologists, and archeologists. Learning and religion have companioned a great deal. On the other hand, one is aware of the so-called war that has gone on between science and religion. Religion, like government, has shown a great need of learning in certain of its creative phases. Once thoroughly established, however, it has tended to guard the "truth" against new data and fresh interpretation. (This, perhaps, should be regarded as a human tendency, not as a specific characteristic of religion.) History records, too, that even scientists sometimes try to obstruct the advance of science.

This war antedates Christianity. There are hymns to wisdom and to thinkers in early Hebrew literature, but there is also the story of the tower of Babel which so clearly shows a distrust of the human mind on the part of established religious institutions. Because of this distrust by established custom and institution Socrates and Servetus and many others died; scholars were intimidated and learning abolished time and again. One of the times when the power of the church was supreme is known to us as the dark ages, although the church was not altogether to blame for that cultural blackout. Even the gentle St. Francis of Assisi, who could outface the devil, was afraid that learning would make inroads on his movement to its detriment.

In my own generation poor Mr. Scopes had to stand trial for teaching elementary science, and currently appearing news items indicate that the quarrel is not over. In our time any vital college professor is an easy target for those who suspect that the minds of youth are being corrupted. At times, this "war" has been waged within the minds of individuals to a sufficient degree to limit seriously their effectiveness as either religionists or intellects. I remember my geology professor once telling of a distinguished past member of his profession who confessed that fossils were to be found on mountaintops all right, but, he contended, they were placed there at the time of creation by God. It would have been argued in those days that the creator did this to test and befuddle the inheritors of human pride and aspiration.

All this can in part be explained in terms of our love for conformity, for we know how in all walks of life deviations even in dress are often ruthlessly censured. I remember a young man of some years ago who candidated for a liberal city church and was so ill-advised as to approach the church edifice on Sunday morning without a hat. For this, although he was otherwise qualified, his name was scratched. Is it any wonder, then, that those holding cherished formulations of the truth, that is, wedded to "sacred" religious practices, should fear the disturbance of new knowledge?

Then the most extraordinary thing happened. A religion appeared that claimed to trust the human reasoning faculty, that abandoned fixed doctrines, that rested its authority upon intelligently interpreted experience, and that laid itself open to constant reconstruction and change while honoring the integrity of the individual. What a promise this movement brought! But even this religion could not quite eliminate the old pattern entirely. The war went on, in some degree, even within the household of liberalism. That this was so can be demonstrated by reference to the treatment given to our now highly esteemed Theodore Parker, who was virtually hounded out of the fellowship by his fellow clerics. I often wonder if this man would be any less disturbing were he living today and pushing his cause in the social context of our time as he did in his own. I am sure that the answer to that wondering is that he would not only be less popular than he is now, being quite dead, but that he would occasion no mean rift in our enlightened Zion. The old weakness is probably still with us, but I have no desire to dwell upon it, for whether it is or not, we have nevertheless courageously avowed faith in the intellect, at times enthroning it above all else. More than this, the most common insistence among us is that we have as individuals, however modest, the right to be governed by our minds. (This seems to me to give greater weight to personal integrity than to reason.) This acceptance of rationality is one of the most significant developments in history, but I suggest that there is more to it than to declare ourselves for the full and free use of reason. When we enthrone reason or anything else, we give it the right to command us in some significant measure, and without appropriate response it loses its significance. Moreover, as hinted above, our individualism suggests that perhaps reason should not be regarded as the cap and crown of our value system. A young Unitarian teacher recently told me that when he listened to a speaker give vehement witness to

26

the primacy of reason in Unitarianism, he immediately shouted "No!" His contention was that the integrity of the self should be regarded as pre-eminent. Fortunately, I don't have to settle this argument for anyone. Our faith offers us a perfect out in facing problems, or I should say in sidestepping problems, which makes the liberal pulpit most attractive. If ministers talk like crazy and get called for it, they are just exercising their right to think for themselves. If they don't know the answers they can always say that their job is to stimulate and the parishioner's job is to find his or her own answers.

But let us set this aside for the moment and address ourselves to the very widespread worship of reason among us, and perhaps see some of the hazards, limitations, and temptations involved. It is my hope to be able to do this in a fellowship devoted to reason, without being branded as a headshrinker. Some of the hazards that dog the steps of those who commit themselves to the authority of reason have already been mentioned. And there are others.

Our clergy share their church bulletins quite freely, and in a recent one I read of one highly respected Unitarian minister preaching on the topic, "How can we get some religion into Unitarianism?" This represents a common internal dissatisfaction with what is considered to be an undue degree of intellectualism, or, perhaps, a too exclusive appeal to reason which apparently leaves a good many of our people cold. A good bit of reasoning never left me cold. I find it, on the contrary, rather exciting, but there *are* those who feel rather clammy in our churches, and they lay the blame on what they call "cold intellectualism." Fear of emotion and sentiment may be responsible, and it is possible that, at times, anything that is just plain boring or outside the context of people's lives, is classifed as intellectual. I used to meet a good many people in our liberal fellowships who actually regarded emotion and sentiment as human weaknesses, and so considered them anathema. Some are still around. Reminding them that they had emotions that required educating, that feeling and sentiment can strengthen and beautify as well as weaken and cheapen, that to hate emotion is to hate oneself, etc., failed to convince them. I suspect that the emphasis on reason would not have earned disrespect, if we had been addicted to the practice as well as to the idea of being rational.

A prominent Unitarian layman who is most loyal to the church says that "a Unitarian church is a haven for people who cannot make up their minds." There is little point in arguing the degree of truth in this statement, but I think it important to note that we tempt people, perhaps, to indecision and the suspension of thinking when we invite them to join us and tell them that we are a creedless church, in which everyone is free to think for himself. The liberal church, like an indulgent foster mother, waits for us and welcomes us with open arms. We achieve self-respect, and freedom from guilt and irritation in those arms, and this is very good as an initial experience. "Come unto me all ye who are bothered by creeds and old religious practices; you are all right as you are." This is fine. There is something redemptive in the acceptance. But for one to remain in that state of innocence is another matter. It may not occur to some that they are making any kind of commitment at all when they walk into those arms. They just sign a book or publicly accept the invitation without word of an imperative of any sort. There is little wonder then that what sometimes happens is that freedom to think is interpreted as the right to be content with the notions and prejudices and convictions already held, many of which are not come by through any intellectual effort. To feel happy with one's unsupported and unexamined convictions without the kind of commitment that might eventually improve upon them may be an innocent and blissful condition, but hardly the fulfillment of liberal promise. On the other hand, we can be proud of the declaration for the right of the individual to think for oneself whether or not one thinks. One begins with this privilege, for which there is a real human need rooted in nature. J. M. Thornburn says, in speaking of art I believe, "All the genuine deep delight of life is in showing people the mud pies you have made; and life is at its best when we confidingly recommend our mud pies to each other's sympathetic consideration." I would not put it that lightly, but the statement does testify to an inborn need, and if our programs catered to it more rather than less we could produce a good deal more than mud pies. As we are, we can be stimulated and hopeful over the wonderful potentiality displayed among us, and at the same time feel despair over the lack of accomplishment in thought.

I feel safe in saying that while we are possibly the knowingest people in the world we, like most modern church groups, know less about religion than about anything else on earth. The proverbial visitor from Mars might expect at least to find bulging libraries in our churches, and most of us making responsible use of them. But if this Martian pursued his studies far enough he might find that instead of committing ourselves to reasoning, we really insist merely upon the privilege of thinking or not, as we choose. Our declarations do not necessarily imply that we should be a company of scholars, but they do imply that we should have the best of scholarly products available, and that we all are actively engaged in the quest to which we say we have a right. We pay a price for giving up popes, creeds, and authoritative books—or don't we?

It is easy also for a faith such as ours to be identified in our minds with ideas currently fresh and widely accepted, or with those we work out for ourselves, and to hold to these as dogmatically as any conservative does to his or her convictions, thus cutting ourselves off from groups with different ideas, and at times, from one another. Some such tension can be found in the most peaceful and cooperative of our congregations. If there isn't a fear of and disrespect for all conservative formulations of thought, there is fear of humanism or social radicalism, and often both fears are housed together. I venture to say that despite our recent progress in this matter there are still liberal clergy who would rather be caught dead than seriously studying the works of living conservative theologians of note.

And now an aside is in order. Experience bedevils me so that I hardly ever contend anything without finding in the very act that something quite contrary is also true, and that one can never correctly characterize people or even oneself without paradoxes and contradictions. The contrary fact here is that many of our clergy do read widely and deeply in the current and classical theology, and I have had the happy surprise of finding old and young people in our churches, from various walks of life, who not only think their religion but read theologians and philosophers. I hope it is apparent that I am not attempting to characterize our people, but rather I am browsing among the vagaries of experience and the temptations and the inadequacies of thought that at times go hand in hand with the most lofty pretensions to thought.

Religion is confronted by problems today if never faced before, such as subtle, hidden, and anonymous forces that influence us, and the impossibility of any group living in isolation again. But there are also the old problems that are forever new, some of which are at the heart of the major crises of the world. So, cutting oneself off from the wisdom of other generations because it is couched in old-time forms will not be without its unhappy consequences. We can, for example, properly repudiate a doctrine such as natural depravity, but we cannot wisely ignore the experience from which it sprang. So, what do *we* do to explain and maybe control the animal impulses—such as those which produced our war-time death camps? How do *we* regard our human insistence on violence in the face of its historic futility? If it isn't natural depravity, what is it? When I raise such questions I am not suffering from a wish to return to the fold or go back to the womb of mother church, but merely suggesting something of what is involved in a commitment to rationality.

I suspect that what light we have on the nature and function of the reasoning capacity needs wider dissemination. It is sometimes assumed that the mind operates independently of glands, muscles, and blood circulation, and of wishes and frustrations, and the like; that it operates quite apart from values. I once read a statement by a somewhat distinguished scientist in which he maintained that we have no business believing in anything, that there's no place for faith and belief for the rational person. I accept his advice enough not to believe him unless and until he can show more evidence. On the contrary I would affirm that even an act of reason is impossible without the involvement of value.

It is quite possible that our reasoning as religionists isn't any better, to put it mildly, than that of the Westminster founders, or the makers of the classic creeds. The difference is in the basic assumptions, and particularly in the values we espouse and for the advancement of which we employ reason. Take, for instance, our belief in our power to redeem ourselves and our world. Is such a conviction rationally derived? It would seem to me that it could be just as rationally determined that the solution of the human problem would be to blast the earth apart and so put an end to it all. But that would be against a built-in urge to live that, unfortunately, only at times uses the mind in its own interest.

It may seem by now that I am, after all, indulging in some head-shrinking, but really all I am attempting is in the interest of rationality. As the saying goes, "It hurts me more than it hurts you." Nothing should stir one more, it would seem to me, than the sight of a real scientist or thinker at work—the breadth of his or her awareness, and the discipline with which one eliminates sources of error, including one's own wishfulness and blind spots. I find no greater cause for faith in the individual. Yet underlying all one does is one's dedicated wish to get at the truth, a tremendously potent value. Julian Huxley says that a scientist, if he is worth his salt (his phrase), has a religious feeling about the truth. So, we may say, values motivate the mind, invent and sustain its disciplines, and enable the thinker to shout "eureka" when the work is successfully done. One of the happiest facts of our faith, in my estimation, is that it accepts and promotes values which are favorable to the free exercise of the mind.

These values do more than motivate inquiry. They provide us with the ends for which we think and, I suspect, at times with the actual stuff *with* which we think. Take, for example, the problem of desegregation confronting our nation. If we despise the racial group involved, and are against ordinary human privileges, how can one's thinking solve the problem short of an extermination policy, and that would be dodging the issue. But let us suppose that we are able to think objectively, to lay aside our prejudices so as to get at the truth. Let us assume that we find Negroes to be just as intelligent, and as capable of ethical sensitivity as any people, and even superior in certain areas such as musical rhythm and harmony and athletics, what can be done with the knowledge if the bias is still there? I once heard a Negro lecturing to college students on this problem. When he was through a young man in the front row asked, "Supposing I grant you all your contentions, and I still don't intend to change my attitude towards Negroes, what are you going to do about *me*?" The question was asked defiantly. The speaker responded after this fashion: "There's nothing that I can do about you. Perhaps some day you may be saved from drowning by a Negro, or carried out of some no-man's-land in some war by a Negro, and then you may want to do something about you, yourself!" I think that answer suggests something of the human condition that affects us all.

This brings to mind one of the greatest of human weaknesses, namely the helplessness of the human mind to make its possessor do even what it clearly indicates he or she should do and he or she wishes to do. The apostle Paul's complaint is a universal one. "That which I would I do not, and that which I would not I do." Nothing so discourages a sensitive soul as this incapacity in people to respond favorably in action to that which is rationally demonstrated as true. We read of a research report, such as a study of the population explosion for example, which clearly sets forth a truth that calls for a change of action. There's no way of dodging or refuting it. If acted upon it would change the direction of the world's cultures, transform persons, and shake up governments. It gets a good review in the journals especially concerned, perhaps a notice in the daily press. In some groups it is passed from hand to hand and is extensively quoted from pulpits and lecterns, and then it meets oblivion or decades pass before anything significant is done. I am here suggesting that the mind's work waits upon values and properly educated emotions for its realization. The human mind is the bit of the iceberg that rises above the surface of the sea. Nevertheless it is part of our glory, despite the fact that some people most endowed with brains have brilliantly served the most unworthy human motives; despite the fact that a brilliantly trained mind can be domesticated by despoilers like any cat or dog.

And so, it seems to me, our liturgical salute to reason and intelligence must be backed by something more than pride in our freedom to be enlightened. I am not at all sure of what we need, but whatever it is it will differentiate between my feeling religious about *my* truth and feeling religiously about truth itself, and I am sure that it will involve a degree of devotion to intelligence in religion which will give us something like a religious discipline. People have often disciplined themselves to the point of self-abuse in the quest for purity and holiness; mortifying the flesh, eliminating worldly distractions ruthlessly in the effort to be personally identified with the faith. The cultures of the world are characterized by customs and mores that were the fruits of rigorous religious discipline. The Amish people, today, deny themselves modern conveniences, defy conventions in clothing, and in general cling to horse-and-buggy days, to keep themselves from being tied in any more with the world. This human motivation is a fact. Isn't there some of it available for our cause, for the support of intelligence in religion? Could the disciplined, creative use of the mind in freedom become as sacred an exercise as prayer used to be? I believe it is possible. I am not an extreme rationalist, but I do think that the development of the human intellect has made it possible for us to believe wisely, and so to reconstruct our beliefs, and that is the distinguishing service that intellectual freedom and training can render to religion.

CHAPTER 5

The Emotional Dimension of Religion

W e need hardly to be convinced of the power and persistence of our emotions. We can be highly rational about them, but we cannot substitute reason for them. At any given time one or the other—that is, reason or emotion—plays a dominant role, but we must never underestimate our capacity for emotional response, or the role of emotion in any act, including the act of reasoning.

I am referring to emotions in the broadest sense—feelings, drives, wants, sentiments, charged values that arise from our inborn needs, and find outlet and function in all we do.

I have been afflicted with half the degenerative diseases known, and am not quite as catty as I used to be. But when I play a certain recording by the Black Watch Bagpipe Band my responses would astonish my friends and, I am sure, alarm my physician. I leap about like a whirling Dervish—enough to kill any ordinary old man, and I have so far taken no hurt. Without the pipes, I think the exertion would kill me. I can look at this phenomenon now quite rationally, and I could even prevent the overt response were I convinced that it would hurt others or kill myself, but I could never prevent the involuntary urgings of my body. If there should be anyone who does not care to label bagpipe sound as music, let one think of one's own beloved form of music and be rational about that, know all about it, discipline oneself and practice making such music until one is an accomplished artist, and music will still be one of the mysteries of one's being, born of a built-in need to respond thus to life at times. Religion is also an expression of human need, and will always remain so. It can be enhanced by the most strenuous application of one's reason, and can thus be made more fruitful, more healing, more beautiful, and less dangerous, but the thing itself will out one way or another. Call it what we will—the finite reaching out for the infinite, as some have put it, or the soul in search of the source whence it came. However one describes it, poetically or scientifically, one cannot explain it away, and it is housed and served by (and serves) feelings, values, sentiments and fancies, hopes, loves, and fears. This is an area in which competent discussions come almost exclusively from the psychiatrists, and to say this is not to underrate the work of theologians. I, as most of us, have been more influenced by the former than the latter, but I shall in no way attempt to represent them here, but speak from the context of my own personal and professional experience.

In some respects, psychiatrists differ about religion almost as much as do theologians. Freud, in his little philosophical work *The Future of an Illusion*, thinks that religion is a liability and should give place to psychoanalysis, something that chains or dwarfs the personality with a crushing measure of infantile dependence. God replaces the parent and so the worshipper is kept a child. This is in his philosophical work. In his clinical reports, I am told by others of his profession, it is not quite the same with him, for in these religion plays a part in the restoration of patients to health. Carl Jung and Otto Rank and others repudiate this fear of religion, and make religion the focal point of their therapy. God is a symbol of psychic energy. Eric Fromm is a Freudian who modifies the views of his master to the point at which he accepts religion and its services as a complement of psychotherapy. He does, however, pass judgement on religion and identifies the good religion with his own humanistic faith. Others, such as Drs. Louis Linn and Leo W. Schwarz, find it necessary and salutary to cooperate with Protestantism, Catholicism, Judaism, or whatever the faith of the patient may be. But no one among the lot questions the deep emotional grounds of religion, and so far as I know not one of note any longer assumes the possibility of its eradication. It is a response to life out of a person's deepest emotional needs.

Could *Homo sapiens* be restored to primitive social condition, all cultures removed as though they had never been, a human being would still be intrigued by sounds, and would soon be thumping rhythmically on a hollow log, or inventing the shepherd's pipe. This being would begin in his or her primitive way to interpret phenomena such as day and night, thunder, sleep, and dreams. Together they would take long looks at their dead companions and begin to offer them some ceremonial tributes—thus expressing their affection perhaps along with the ritualistic performance of each one's own last rites—and, before too many millennia, they would people the earth and heavens with gods and jinns and devils, and begin to represent these in symbols: material, ceremonial, and conceptual; symbols that would speak to their deepest needs, hopes and fears. Even in our so-called advanced stage of culture such symbols remain, reaching many people more deeply than any rational interpretation of them could justify. It is not any great mystery that the crescent moon should serve desert peoples as a God, in their night travel for water or pasturage, or that the sun should become the God of gods and the precursor of monotheism, or that when the aspirations of human beings transcended their culture and many were killed for their pains, the cross, an instrument of death, should become one of the world's most sacred symbols.

One of the strongest individual needs is to find some meaningful interpretation of life and the universe. When these explanations come they carry values, for the meanings are not sought out of idle curiosity. Even the most primitive of religious concepts, mana, has been interpreted as "the thing that matters most," i.e., the highest in the scale of values. These meanings have always been related to a person's well-being whether we refer to the primitive god of thunder or to Nirvana. At least one distinguished therapist bases his therapy on the need for meaning. This inner need is so strong that when one cannot actually know, as we conceive of knowing today, one creates answers imaginatively out of the urgency of spirit and limited experience. The individual is not happy within the bounds of the known, or of even the knowable, and so theologians, mystics, poets, philosophers, musicians, science fiction writers, etc., come into being.

It is no wonder that the universe was peopled with beings born of the human mind and imagination. After many millennia, humans began to be directed in part by what we call conscience, and Mr. J. A. Breasted assures us that that was a very short time ago, not more than five thousand years. Thus the law began to be written on the human heart, and thus was furthered one's sense of being, one's sense of integrity and personal sovereignty, and this in turn probably led to the birth of freedom.

Human beings had need of love and warmth and intimacy, and

since these were among the dear realities of life, the gods began to acquire warmth and concern for humans until finally the one and only God did not deal with people according to their deserts, and so the great theological concepts of mercy and grace and love were born.

But religion has not been as salutary as it has been inescapable. It naturally caught up human limitations as well as virtues, weaknesses as well as strengths, vindictiveness and sadism as well as love and forgiveness, divisiveness as well as hunger for unity. And there was little hope of its improvement, until the individual acquired powers of discrimination. The further evolution of religion waited upon the development of the reasoning faculty and for the accumulation of centuries of recorded human experience, on which the mind could work. Some of the most valuable fruits of reason come today from those who have explored the human psyche. And there is an astonishing unanimity among those whose works I happen to know about the earmarks of what they call mature religion; that is, the religion of a healthy person. The mature religious sentiment, they say, displays a capacity to love and be loved, independence, uniqueness, a sense of integrity in thought and act, responsibility, and involvement in the reduction of human suffering, and, of course, the freedom that all these require. If these be the measures of a mature person's religion, then they are also the characteristics of the religion that should cater to human needs, and they represent to an astonishing degree the ethical core of the world's great religions, and particularly the claims of liberal religion.

Eric Fromm defines religion as a system of thought and action characteristic of a group which gives the individual a "frame of reference and an object of devotion."[2] He further contends that any satisfying system of orientation implies not only intellectual elements, but elements of feeling and sense to be realized in action in all fields of human endeavor, and that devotion to an aim, or an idea, or a power transcending man such as God is an expression of this need for completeness in the process of living. But, as we have seen, religion, like all human enterprises, needs eternal re-evaluation and refinement. History, and history now in the making, display plenty of the crudities and dangers associated with religion. The progressive elimination of such dangers will come not by reason alone but by reason in response to the protests of the human heart that is outraged by doctrines and practices that do not serve it. The hurt is a clue to the false in religion. The individual will not grow or improve, for example, on a religion of fear, despite the Scottish poets' view that "the fear o' hell is the hangman's whup to haud the wretch in order." We need only remember the years when we used to see rows of white crosses at highway and railway intersections, or crosses along the way recording that here and there so many had died. They are now all gone, for the record is that giving the appearance of a cemetery to an intersection in no way deters the reckless. Fear's hazards are many; its salutary effects few and questionable.

We have noted that the human species, in the course of evolution, developed a sense of independence and integrity. The individual became in a measure sovereign, and acquired uniqueness of mind and personality. To this whole tendency in his or her being the creeds have been an affront, and they have been powerless whenever the individual achieved real significance as people. All the great leaders were characterized by this uniqueness, from Moses and the other prophets to Jesus and Luther and Calvin and Zwingli and Schweitzer and Gandhi or the Buddha—or whom does one care to mention? Creative capacity is an expression of this uniqueness.

We can say the same of any local church leader who is worth his or her salt, whether or not of a credal church. We take this and discard that, and this is how we wish to make our peace with life. And remember, this is no wholesale attack on creeds. They probably served more than one real purpose while confining the individual spirit.

This fact of individual uniqueness calls for the continuous reconstruction of religions. It has been begging for attention throughout the centuries, and is only now being recognized as something to which religion, and states, must eventually cater, which they must honor and find use for. And what is it? Surely not just a rational capacity without a drive. The most significant thing about it is the drive. Humans seek to be self-directing, to put their own label on truth. This may get them into a hornet's nest of new problems, but it is so, nevertheless.

We may have leaned too far in a justifiable fear of creeds—at times to the point where we wish not to inquire after meanings at all, or attempt an assessment of our common faith. The Universalists through the years developed the habit of periodically reviewing beliefs they held in common. This had the value of disclosing common concerns without binding anyone and, as they claimed, did not fall into the category of creed.

As a matter of fact, Christianity and Judaism and Buddhism have in their classic statements recognized that the individual must seek the truth, but this awareness has been honored in the breach more

37

than otherwise. And this is not all. Almost every great religion has also displayed a yearning for the unity of humankind. Although they never got anywhere in the achievement of unity, the recognition of the need was there. Expressions of hope that all Protestants can get together sometime, that Catholics, both Roman and Greek, and Episcopalians can find a common communion, etc., can be found in the records of church councils right up to the present time. The aggressive desire of some religions to convert the world may be a form of this desire, even if, perhaps, a perverted one. And all this yearning for unity calls for a religion with a much greater intellectual capacity and emotional maturity than we seem to have yet acquired. This is an aspiration that belongs to the human personal structure, and it will somewhat condition the work of the brain to the end of time.

So I could go on. Human beings have a nature. This is the basis of Camus' objection to Fascist and Marxist ideologies. They do not recognize an individual's nature. Some of us have called attention to this fault in religions for many years. One's need of religion and one's responses to what it does for one suggests its refinement. We have heard of doctrines such as the damnation of unbaptized infants. I once had an encounter with a cleric who came to the home in which I lived to baptize an ailing infant and who, on finding the child already dead, threw up his arms and exclaimed, "This child is lost." The mother's hurt indicated that he was the lost one, and the verdict of history is already for her. Churches have at times regarded certain sins, such as that against the holy spirit, as unpardonable, and this doctrine too was discredited by what it did to people. Religion must accommodate itself to our inborn emotional needs. One can reason oneself to the point where one can justify almost anything, and theologians are especially clever at this art, but one cannot in the long run make an outrageous doctrine acceptable to the human heart. So in a devious way I have tried to indicate the depth and constructive strength of emotion in religion. I would like to turn now to the more direct evidence of our own experience.

I preach at times and some of my sermons have been called lectures. I see nothing wrong with a lecture, if it is a good one, but in so characterizing a sermon there may be an implicit judgment of it as being okay intellectually, but lacking in warmth and appeal, and if this is so, the judgment is justifiable. We do want the truth wrapped in personal warmth and intimacy of experience, especially truth that is hard to take. There is no tendency at this point to forget that warmth and intimacy and balderdash or falsehood can be dangerous when wedded together. I find in my experience as a teacher, and more recently as a preacher, that the most accurate of statements pass over most people's heads when they are devoid of beauty and warm intimacy or something else that speaks to one's feelings. Truths are not only more understandable, when addressed to the heart as well as the head, but often more usable; more easily possessed as personal assets—life's natural and unhappy limitations, for instance. And let me be my own horrible example again. I worry about my problems a great deal—an obnoxious habit—and often I am told the truth about the foolishness of worrying about difficulties—"worry never helped," and so on. All these well-intended ministrations made not the slightest difference, despite their undeniable truth. Then, one day, I happened to read Robert Frost's poem, about the tree that fell across the road:

> The tree the tempest with a crash of wood
> Throws down in front of us is not to bar
> Our passage to our journey's end for good,
> But just to ask us who we think we are.[3]

I read this and added some profane refinements for emphasis, and all my worries looked silly, and for some days I actually loved my problems. When in real difficulty I still go back to it, just to be asked who I think I am anyway. Why do I respond this way while I am unmoved by a factual statement of my condition? Well, I ask you. Although I cannot explain why, I regard such experiences as most healthy as well as highly religious.

I feel somewhat the same about some of the traditional religious concepts. The concept of God, for instance, is born of an emotional need, as I am sure the drive to repudiate it is also. There is a need to relate to the universe and source of life. The concept of God did not develop, I feel, out of a craving for a father image or sovereign idea, before which to grovel and remain a child. It has been so used at times—and here's a fact Freud should have noted—children do not want to grovel to begin with. Neither did the originator of the God idea. It has just as strong an appeal to the creative emotions. One wants to relate oneself in both feeling and thought to the totality of all things. To question any particular formulation of the reality to which one seeks to respond is highly justifiable, but to question the yearning in the face of history would be difficult for a mind both informed and free. I have myself gone through many stages of belief from naive faith to intellectual belief, to doubt, to repudiation, to negation, to the point where I conceived of the universe as a great mechanism spiralling and whirling its way through eternity with complete indifference to me, and to the point eventually of some sense of dynamic unity and oneness and a sustaining measure of happiness and a reluctant acceptance of mortality and all it entails. The creative discovery for me was that no matter how indifferent the universe might be to me I could not be indifferent to it, and that this compulsion of mine was also of the universe—more really so than is the machine I use to write these words. I may have never come closer to God than Wordsworth did in his moment of elevated thought, but then, in the feeling that I belong to the universe, I never got very far away either. The fact that I belonged consoled me, even when the hope of immortality died. This is not intellectual comprehension of the truth. It is a poetic acceptance of the inevitable and a poetic or spiritual fulfillment as necessary to me as my morning's oatmeal. I recently read an article in *Natural History* magazine, in which an experiment with monkeys deprived of natural mothering was described. They were given mannikin mothers or deprived entirely, and the result was severe neuroses. Some people experience the universe as a kind of unresponsive mannikin mother. I think I have escaped that, and one of the tasks of religion is to help people escape it.

My favorite poet speaks of writing poems in order to produce not always explicit truths, but the "sound of meaning." Anyone who can understand that can have some understanding of the kingdom in which I live. The sound of meaning, the sense of meaning, when nothing better serves—I have been elevated by it, humbled by it, have been driven by it to dancing and laughter and tears, and I have lived by it after the mind, doing its darndest, had come to grinding away, without grist. And it has elevated the fruitful act of thought no less.

I conceive of theology as a divine art, and I am most conscious of the fact that there is such a thing as poetic behavior as well as poetry. So I hope that the next stage in the development of religion will be to conceive of theology as an art, for I believe that an art can be as liberating and as creative as the scientific method, and if so recognized, theology's pretensions might come to be more in line with what is possible for it to accomplish. Theology's service to us, whether it be theistic, agnostic, or atheistic, is not merely intellectual. It releases our capacity for devotion, and even though it be devoid of a God concept, devotion is still enhanced, given its object more clearly, and so its disciplines.

This sense of oneness with life that we may feel, this sense of kinship, this elevation of thought and aspiration, this refusing to remain within the limits of the fully grasped or the rationally demonstrated in no way corrupts the mind for its careful observation and interpretation of empirical data. I find that when I am most moved, my mind is most active, and even most trustworthy. For example, how easy it is for the liberal to think of the universe as an impersonal and purposeless, and unconscious mechanism. It seems so obvious, so commonsense a notion. Yet out of my sheer love of persons and life, my love of the universe and my desire to talk to it, came the realization that in interpreting the universe as mentioned above we project merely what we know about chemistry and physics and astronomy, and completely overlook that which we regard as most precious: consciousness, mind, personality. While projecting out of experience, as we must, why not project such things? I have heard hard-boiled rationalists talk endlessly on this general subject without ever becoming conscious of the theological problem that personality creates for the liberal, and without apparent awareness of the fact that in us the universe became alive and conscious and concerned. So my mystical inclinations have clarified my mind on this problem rather than clouding it. And, please, I am not suggesting that God must be a person, but merely throwing a tree across the road at a point where we need to be asked a question by life in exchange for all the questions we ask of it.

This is all very personal and intimate, and I have found it necessary to make it so. I would be shy of making such statements were it not for the danger of missing the spirit of religion in the very act of discussing it. Above all else I wished to counter the notion that emotions are traps and agencies by which we may be exploited. They carry such danger, but so does reasoning. Think of what Hitler did to the brains of Germany, or of what the world is doing to brains now. A scientist in his or her lab can be as much adrift from the world and as unaware of the consequences of his or her own acts as any monk in his cell. We can never dodge dangers; we have to learn to deal with them. Life will not be ordered for us. We shall never escape the necessity of striving to ensure that the religious spirit within us, as St. Paul said, is not "the spirit of fear, but the spirit of power, of love, and of a sound mind."[4]

CHAPTER 6

The Give-and-Take of Love: The Basic Religious Relationship

We emphasize thinking for ourselves, and seeking the truth, and good human relations, and these call for a measure of spiritual health, or, as we more commonly say, emotional maturity. We sense here at once a hen-and-egg situation. Real studiousness and good human relations begin with the self, and the wholesome self requires wholesome human contacts. The thing to remember is that the hen and the egg are both real. Soul health is relative, no doubt, as I intend to show. I am sure self-reliance isn't what we often think it is. Therapists have probably told us enough about it, but we have to incorporate this wisdom of our era in the practice of the faith we serve.

On the necessity of respecting oneself, of loving oneself, there is no better statement than the popular one by Carl Jung.

In actual life, it requires the greatest discipline to be simple, and the acceptance of one's self is the essence of the moral problem and the epitome of a whole outlook on life. That I feed the hungry, that I forgive an insult, that I love my enemy in the name of Christ—all these are undoubtedly great virtues. What I do unto the least of my brethren, that I do unto Christ. But what if I should discover that the least amongst them all, the poorest of all the beggars, the most impudent of all the offenders, the very enemy himself—that these are within me, and that I myself stand in need of the alms of my own kindess—that I myself am the enemy who must be loved—what then? As a rule, the Christian's attitude is then reversed;

43

there is no longer any question of love or long suffering; we say to the brother within us, "Raca," and condemn and rage against ourselves. We hide it from the world, we refuse ever to admit having met this least among the lowly in ourselves. Had it been God Himself who drew near to us in this despicable form, we should have denied him a thousand times before a single cock had crowed.

Are we to understand the "Imitation of Christ" in the sense that we should copy his life and, if I may use the expression, ape his stigmata; or in the deeper sense that we are to live our own proper lives as truly as he lived his in all its implications? It is no easy matter to live a life that is modelled on Christ's, but it is unspeakably harder to live one's own life, as truly as Christ lived his.[1]

Thus Jung corrects an almost masochistic strain of self-abasement in the Christian tradition. We can be fooled, however, by old language in interpreting that tradition generally. The self-surrender recommended in many cases was the surrender of fear and dependence, and the sense of one's own limitations which were lost in the feeling that one was given to the service of the Almighty. Nevertheless, Jung's analysis is probably more correct than in error. Anyway, without strength of soul, we utilize but a fraction of one's potential as a being—one cannot love others; unsure and worried about one-self, one's civic efforts are worried and fearful; the vocation by which one makes one's living suffers from uncertainty and frustration; opportunity may approach us blowing a trumpet and wearing a fore-lock a yard long, but the individual cannot grasp it. I once knew a man who fell in love with a girl, and although she responded to him, he abandoned her out of a sense of his own unworthiness. This suggests how wormish a person can get. Also, I am sure that the standoffish stance adopted by some who can find little or nothing that is good in the world stems from this weakness. The current fear over one's ability to keep one's soul which is reflected in poetry, drama, fiction, and philosophy represent the problem in its widest and deepest aspects.

So, without any more argument, let us assume that self-love or self-reliance is a good thing. *But how does one come by it? And how does one maintain the essential sense of worth?* There is no use at all in preaching about it to people, or in giving them books on its desirability. Such efforts may have no greater results than to accentuate self-abasement.

It is possible that some are born with a toughness of fiber that enables them to go it alone better than others, but I am sure that the mature sense of being is so loaded with experience that for the present purpose we can forget what we were born with. It is also true, in a sense, that we achieve this strength of being on our own, but we know that circumstances can make such achievement very difficult or impossible. So we can assume, too, that circumstances can make it possible. Even children in our church schools now know of how newly born infants can be saved from death by loving, fondling care when medicine alone cannot save them. In view of this I recall with horror the discipline of the "twenties" when infants were trained to eat, sleep, wake up, and use the toilet by the clock. When they cried they were left to howl until exhaustion overwhelmed them. These, I may add, were the children of those most informed on the latest in child nurture. I remember one mother who gave her child the same meal four times without succeeding in making him eat it, but on the fifth try at the end of his second day of fasting, he did eat it. And a fact that may have in it a corrective for our permissive times is that this child was never twisted in personality or health, and is now a rather distinguished professional man—which may be because he had an abundance of affection despite the battle over the spinach.

The fact seems to be that affection and respect and concern for persons are basic to physical recovery, and that adults and the aged respond physically to such ministrations as well as infants, even in extremities of great illness, and that such giving of one's self to another contributes to an even greater degree to the keeping of one's own soul (or psyche) in health. I have not the slightest doubt about this. And this has an intimate connection with the whole business of being and doing good.

I have observed an intimate chain of close, affectionate relations throughout one's whole span of life that seems to me to be far from insignificant. First, we are watched over with affection and concern and caressed by our parents, and when we leave them we, for better or worse, cleave unto another. Then when old age overtakes us, and the old person's oft-repeated tales are hard to listen to, and he or she is increasingly set apart and in danger of losing the will to live, there is the grandchild who loves this person deeply, and to whom he or she can give love again no less needed. Find a person without any of these relations and you find one who is living at a disadvantage or is living on a very favorable bank balance of love and respect received. To live without anyone who thinks of us as important is to make existence a heartbreaking endurance trial. I am deeply conscious of what we owe the great men and women, not just for what they did, but for what they were. They all were much involved in our aspirations, and in our self-images and visions of what ought to be. But I also know that this self-reliance or health of soul which permits us to live and love and work is deeply rooted in the services of love and respect we receive from those with whom we live and work. I am one of those unfortunates who must confess to having walked a terrible road to some sustaining measure of self-assurance. I have to confess also that I would still be much farther back on that road were it not for the people who loved me, who believed in me without much cause and loved me just for me, who expected good things of me and trusted me, and whom I could trust with my name, honor, and—I will not say fortune, for a good and sufficient and private reason.

I remember a parish that had always been served by theological seminary students and in which the people bragged constantly about the fact that those who had served them as novitiates in the ministry had nearly all become distinguished in some way or other. They dinned this into my ears when I served them, and took it for granted that I was destined at least to become the head of a theological seminary, something a number of my predecessors had achieved, little realizing how they tended to determine whatever distinction one might achieve.

I suspect that you might remember, as I do, when our young eyes looked into older eyes and saw there an image of ourselves, and what a difference it made whether that image was something less significant than we had thought of ourselves, or reflected something much more worthy and hopeful and wonderful than we ever dared to identify with ourselves. I have often noticed how many male authors give their wives credit, and I am sure many of these are most sincere. It is probably not because the wife read the manuscript or did typing, but because she saw him bigger than he was and he grew on that vision of hers.

In our competitive business culture we are prone to accentuate the sturdy qualities, and perhaps so much so that at times we forgive a good deal of wrongdoing and incompetence and foolishness because of them, and we are prone to forget their roots, especially since we rule out sentiment and personal considerations and sometimes ethical considerations, in dealing with them.

Let us assume that we are sufficiently self-reliant persons. Well, I maintain that we are not *always* so, and also that in certain areas of life we may not be so at all. Wasn't it Georgie Porgie who was terrific with the girls and couldn't make his way with the boys at all? The great he-man who has a horror of death is not hard to find. Nor is the timid one who becomes a giant when his back is to the wall. I can't help recalling here an anxious and troubled person I know who gets a new lease on life behind the wheel of an automobile, and drives with the boldness and skill that might make the toughest taxi driver envious. I can, on the contrary, face up to some difficult situations, but behind the wheel of a car I am almost the proverbial "Milquetoast," constantly being edged out by the bold ones.

There are times, occasions, areas, in which we are strong, and there are times and places where it is hazardous for us to go it alone. That is why, in my opinion, the church could be of immeasurable service to us as individuals, if it could but partly live up to what I envision for it. I may be just a visionary, but I do not think it beyond us as a church to have support for one another in our low moments, and, on the other hand, have outlets for strength when and where we are strong.

Today you may be griefstricken, and I, being less immediately involved in the tragedy of our mortality, can stand by you. Tomorrow I will need you in this or an equally trying circumstance. A neighbor's time of final separation has come, and you stand by him or her on the brink of life, and maybe hold a hand, embarrassed by your own impotence. Yet you go away better prepared for the day when the bells toll for you by the display of quiet courage that your own ministrations partly inspired. Today I am, perhaps, maligned, falsely accused, or I may be misunderstood and fenced about with accusing, suspicious eyes, and there is nothing on earth I need so much as someone who believes me. Who has not been in such a spot is fortunate indeed. It's a common experience with children, and not unknown to us when grown. On the other hand, I may be quite guilty of betraying my best self and the public mores, and I need forgiveness, and may have little chance of recovery without it. Who's around to meet my need? There is also the day when misfortune and frustration make me feel like betraying my faith—I want to curse God and die, and I very much need your strength, or I am fearful and need your courage. Or I am so blinded by treachery and hurt that I cannot think logically and I shout for vengeance, and I so much need your wider perspective on things, your present grasp of wisdom. Tomorrow you will need me, or someone, for such days are commonly experienced. There are times when we cannot be decent even to our families, or when the family is the only place in which we have the courage to be nasty. There are times when we fumble the day's work and get the censure we earn. At such times we are among the "little ones" whom no one had better offend, if one does not wish to merit the millstone and the deep blue sea.

Fortunately, there are often people who see us through. There are also the days and circumstances of our strength when others falter, and we have an excess of what it takes that we may share. If I am wrong in all this, I have greatly misjudged people with whom I live, and greatly misinterpreted my own life.

I flatter myself naively with the idea or hope that we have a "treasury of merit" among us. There is the old doctrine that saints out of their excess of goodness have laid up in Heaven a treasury of merit from which sinners less happily situated can draw to make up their own deficits, and thus merit forgiveness and Heaven. A lot of nonsense this may seem until we sense its poetic truth and its practical possibilities. How beautifully it symbolizes what I am trying to say. It is my conviction that there has always been this ministry of people for people, and that it has always been more important than anything else, even as part of the services a minister renders. I think this is what the theologians call common grace, but why it isn't also the grace of God is not too clear to me. In this connection I have lost most of my capacity to differentiate between people as saints and sinners, wise or foolish, weak or strong. Those of us who have had war experience have seen the very model of virile manhood cringe and cry so as to draw contempt, while others who bore the label of insignificance took their places and made up for what they lacked. We have known the most erudite to act like morons, and do so habitually in certain areas of life. We have known illiterates to live with such wisdom as we associate only with the greatest souls. We have known the "sinner" to be the first at our door when trouble hits us. So I am inclined to drop all labels. Anyway, once, we label people, we respond to those labels, and never get to know or serve those who wear them. We all possess enough virtues and vices to merit one another's respect and compassion. This is my reason for expecting so much from a church. I wonder, if we disciplined ourselves enough, if we could experiment enough with good will to discover its power—would the wrong doer or the falsely accused have a better chance among us than elsewhere? The woman who was about to be stoned in the gospel story—how would she fare? Could a person be discredited among us by sheer unfounded gossip less easily than in most places? Can a young one growing up among us experience a sense of worth more easily for the company we provide? Would our corporate, as well as personal, life make such an impact upon the young that they would not doubt the church's power and value? We cannot expect to find a company of saints in any church, but it doesn't take a saint to do what I have in mind. In fact, I feel the saints could do less than the dedicated imperfect in the sharing of what our souls need. At any rate, the church should be a place where we could more easily put our best foot forward, even if we have to drag a reluctant cloven hoof behind.

The point of all this is that we possess a rather terrifying power over one another. Some people have a great redemptive gift. They redeem people from their worst impulses and from the consequences of their acts. They redeem the day, the hour, and the circumstances, and the institutions they serve often take on new life. One feels better when he passes such a one on the street. There are those also who, unfortunately, have acquired out of the distortion of their own souls an equally destructive power and skill, and happy are those who have not met up with their kind. But I am not thinking of extremes, but of common gifts and failings. I can acknowledge the life-giving power of a shouted greeting from a four-year-old from across the street, or in the wag of a dog's tail, and no one needs training to smell the vial of poison that can be hidden in a bouquet of sweet words. Perhaps this power is most easily demonstrated by our influence on animals. In my family we once had our children experiment with love therapy on a stray homeless cat that was as emaciated and ugly and nasty as a creature could be after being kicked from door to door all winter. At first he slashed one's arms when picked up, but in a very few weeks he would cuddle in a lap and purr and sit up in his natural beauty and dignity. The recovery of poise and beauty was most impressive.

I hope the following story will not seem too silly and personal. I had had one of those unfortunate days when everything goes dead wrong. My wife was away and the house was a mess; the car would not start and I had to walk to work. On my way, I met a man I had greatly admired and had not seen in years and greeted him warmly. He was puzzled, so I told him who I was, "Oh yes," he said, "MacLean, of course. I must have met you somewhere," and he took off. My morning's lecture at school was a flop and one student wasn't afraid to say so. I was also out of funds and I had to go to the bursar's office for an advance on my salary. His secretary shouted my request like a circus barker, and I walked between desks aflame with the consciousness that all and sundry knew that I was in want. On my way home I remembered the dog I had forgotten and left unfed and confined all day. I entered the house with a burden of guilt added to frustrations and embarrassments, and there on the rug on the hall floor was the dog, eyes twinkling, and his great plume waving as though he were fully aware of my lapse and was making allowances. Then he sprang at me in greeting. The whole burden of the awful day was immediately lifted from me and I felt whole again. Thus I would accent the life-and-death power we have over one another. I have written of this dimension of experience not to encourage anyone to lean on his or her neighbor. What one can and should do towards the making and saving of one's own soul is partly here by implication. I do wish to indicate how many things we receive as free gifts which we cannot buy, borrow, steal, or command, and upon which our strength and happiness depend. It is very necessary that people get some sense of their own worth, and I think this comes better along with a realistic awareness of our interdependence. We are in one another's hands, and whether or not these can be God's hands depends upon how we use a God-given power.

Yet I have another purpose, too. While I have been directly talking of what we owe to others in the matter of health and sturdiness of spirit I have also been indicating how to be and do the truth. The difficulties are enormous. Try loving your enemy! It's quite possible though. We have difficulty enough in meeting minor obstacles within ourselves and in the behavior of others. But there is this about it all; the life of mutuality and love I have been talking about provides us with the greatest degree of assurance and life confidence that we shall ever acquire. One doesn't love in order to reap the benefits of loving, but it pays off just the same. In personal relations, we at least know pretty well what we should do, or, I should say, *can* know what to do. It is far from being so in other areas where real puzzlements are added to our imperfections, as we shall see.

The point is that there is no real self without the other. We have made a fetish of individualism without understanding its source and strength. I am afraid that the world's problems await our increased maturity in this area, and yet that maturity cannot come in isolation from the world's problems.

CHAPTER 7

The Dream of a Redeemed Society

W hat of the dream of saving society, and of finding fulfillment in a "saved" society? Something has gone wrong with it, and this, whatever it be, is probably a principal source of the spiritual frustration and the sense of personal ineffectualness that infects so many. I suspect that it has more to do with the philosophies of despair and cynicism than is generally recognized. I know very little about it, but I have to size it up for myself before I can go on with the business of doing good as a member of a corporate society. I have lived long enough to know that something serious has happened even if I had read nothing of the fears and anger that have been voiced in the world. Something has happened to our hopes and dreams for a renewed, a "redeemed" society. The very idea of the future seems to be without invitation or promise, except for private enterprises. The Christian dream of a cataclysmic divine intervention has been gone for a long time for us, even the idea of a Christianized world. The dream of the twenties—the hope of routing the robber barons, of finding the devils and destroying them, is gone. Even the dream of the life of abundance that has been the popular appeal from the institutions of our economic system, although amply realized, has brought disillusionment, a disillusionment more destructive than the frustration associated with personal morality. The English poet George Barker wonders how he can be happy when he knows it can be only for here and now.

And listen to this from W. H. Auden in "In Time of War."

> He turned his field into a meeting place,
> And grew the tolerant ironic eye,
> And formed the mobile money-changer's face,
> And found the notion of equality.
>
> And strangers were as brothers to his clocks,
> And with his spires he made a human sky;
> Museums stored his learning like a box,
> And paper watched his money like a spy.
>
> It grew so fast his life was overgrown,
> And he forgot what once it had been made for,
> And gathered into crowds and was alone,
>
> And lived expensively and did without,
> And could not find the earth which he had paid for,
> Nor feel the love that he knew all about.[1]

This speaks to me of my theme even if it is possible that I do not understand it as the poet did. He might have spoken too of the things we feel and are influenced by and about which we know nothing at all. The dreams of corporate salvation—Christian, Socialist, Marxist, industrial—have lost their power to move our souls. And one without a dream that sweetens and motivates life has nightmares of outlanders' aggression, or loss of soul in totalitarian society, or of sudden death to all.

I suspect that the irreducible element in one's dreaming tendency is a vague expectancy, an anticipation of good things that give life its zest, and makes us observant and responsive as we never can be when this mood is absent. We sometimes walk the woods and stride the hills when stones and grasses and the birds of the air are just things that ask no questions, tease no sense of wonder from us, nor find any warm response in us. But there are times when we rise to meet the morning as though we had never seen a sunrise, and, in a sense, it may turn out that we haven't. There are invitations in the air and all about us, and we accept them exultantly. We listen to the winds tuning up the leaves for their day's performance, the hills and the headlands seem to shout us welcome, and meandering paths lure our feet where they will, and we are never disappointed as we turn back home. I have known people to respond to books this way, fondling them with the tenderest anticipation, and happy is the author whose books fall into such hands. Some for whom the song birds sing in vain will turn to auction sales, secondhand stores, old furniture, and even junk heaps as though about to experience complete fulfillment. Some rare souls respond to people this way, and they are rarely disappointed. People come out of hiding for them. Some undertake the daily task this way, and it is to these that labor yields its exceptional rewards.

Probably out of this capacity for anticipation, spurred by mortal pains and frustrations, the great dream evolves, takes form, and gathers about it man's fondest hopes, faith, and purposes, and commands his energies and capacities as nothing else can.

The waxen wings of Daedalus and Icarus are a long way from the modern jet-liner, but they belong together, and man's inner urge to fly finds new expression in the spaceways. In the fields of science, the parallels are legion, perhaps in a most significant way in medicine. There are countless life stories in which dreams of doing the impossible were actually realized and many who failed nevertheless made it possible for their successors to succeed.

These are the fruitful dreams. There are dreams that people cannot follow. I think of the proverbial tramp who dreams of someday picking up a fortune in the streets. I recall also a novel, read many years ago, that told the story of a young man who lived with a profound sense of destiny. He had been in the navy throughout World War I. Three ships on which he served were torpedoed one after another with only a few surviving. On the last one he was the lone survivor. No wonder he felt that he had been spared for great things, and that he was filled with a sense of something tremendous impending. Well, he did survive and got back home to the Middle West, fell in love with a nice girl, and settled down to a life-long career as a clerk in the A & P. Some dreams are not backed by ability or character, but they are not insignificant, nevertheless.

I remember hearing a Czech speak of his peoples' history right after World War I when his country became a democracy. He spoke of folk songs and stories and customs and festivals in which the hopes of his people had lived for generations while they bowed their necks to foreign yokes. When songs and festivals that have achieved the status of real folk art sponsor a people's cause, that cause is not likely to be forgotten. It will live on until the day of opportunity arrives. I am sure that all this has not escaped the totalitarian dictators, and may very well explain their interest in directing and controlling the arts. They may even have gotten the idea from Plato, who also thought it was in the interest of the state to control the arts. Our future depends much on whether or not the arts can be directed and controlled. I suspect that they cannot, for they have a subtlety that can both deceive and outface tyranny, even though their patient waiting may cover hundreds of years. Although the American Negroes were so tightly controlled that their spirits could only sing of sweet chariots, or share in the poet Johnson's hope that on resurrection day the grave of the unknown soldier in Arlington Cemetery would open and out would come a giant Negro man singing "Glory" as he started his march to Heaven, their aspiration still lived undiminished in its strength and ready for opportunity. That dream is now becoming purpose and commitment to specific action. And perhaps the gentleness with which these people seize upon their opportunity is born of the gentleness of their dreams. Who knows but they will add to the world's meagre experience the classic instance of a great revolution without great violence.

But together we shared a great dream, and it has been disrupted. Why? In *A Study of History,* the indefatigable Mr. Toynbee has produced a monumental work that in erudition and scope must make old Gibbon have qualms about his place in history. I confess that my knowledge of this work has not come from reading the many volumes that contain it, but from commentaries, lengthy reviews, and symposia which are sufficient for my present modest purpose. In his analysis Toynbee finds that civilizations live and die according to an historically determined pattern. Our Western culture, he thinks, is now at a stage when it has its last chance for self-renewal. We strive, he believes, for self-determination in our corporate life as in personal life. We envisions a world-to-be, and our eneregies are geared thereto. All living civilizations strive to transform the cities of the world into the city of God. They embody purpose in pursuit of a great vision. The successful civilization, therefore, is the one that is progressively unique, ever recapturing the needed vision in new terms. The declining civilization is the one that is progressively and increasingly uniform. When a culture like Rome's comes to the point when its task is to put the empire in order, as Augustus conceived of his mission, it is already doomed to death. In times of crisis the great need is to restore a society to unity and effort by a transforming vision. The saving element in a society is to gain a new perspective on tradition and purpose, to create a new religion, a higher religion, and the transforming vision of this religion turns death to life, and sets a civilization on the way to fresh fulfillment. By recreating the future it is granted survival.

Americans generally will respond negatively, as I do, to some of the details of Toynbee's analysis—to his conviction, for instance, that only the very few can have saving visions, and that all the rest

54

of us follow them like sheep. Also to his insinuation that a state's concern with order, social legislation, the meeting of material needs such as a high standard of living, and preoccupation with science and technology are indications of approaching degeneracy and death. I like his recognition of the role of the vision or dream, but I don't like his particular vision, which smacks a bit of medievalism.

In *The Case for Modern Man*,[2] Charles Frankel, the Columbia University philosopher, takes the erudite Toynbee pretty well apart on this issue, likening his argument to blaming arithmetic for Junior's troubles in school. Nevertheless, Frankel's own analysis and arguments are quite in line with the basic conviction I express here. "The simple fact is," he says, "that men's happiness depends upon their expectations." While opening our eyes to the great values in our culture, he does not give it a clean bill of health. He thinks that there is something definitely wrong with it. One of these things that threaten our sense of security is *the social power that is wielded anonymously in our society,* that is, by people who release instruments of power without awareness of their social consequences, and, of course, without the sense of social responsibility that such awareness might engender. He says that if these people came dressed in the garb of social planners we would regard them as tyrants, for their basic social decisions bypass the traditional public discussion and consent on which we always have supposed major social decisions should rest. People feel impotent, and they half suspect that they are being manipulated by invisible persons of power they do not know and cannot control. While Frankel's argument is quite the reverse of a condemnation of our technology and industrialism or free enterprise he says, "Technological developments have eaten out the social texture of modern society," greatly depleting the power of the community, church, and home. So our access to centers of power, to the control and direction of society are increasingly remote and abstract. He says further,

Such changes in our institutions are the sort of thing which threatens to engulf the liberal image of a society made up of men who set their own standards, run their own lives, and cooperate as equals in dealing with common problems. The overhanging problem for contemporary liberals— a problem which challenges their courage and intelligence, and most of all their imaginations—is this drift of decision-making authority, into key positions that are anonymous, the development of an institutional structure that denies the individual genuine options, and the increasing inadequacy of our inherited mechanisms of public discussion and consent to control the situation.[3]

All this, he adds, is not oligarchy, not economic exploitation. It is not many things of ill repute with which it has been identified. At the same time, he says, *it is not what has been envisioned by modern liberal democracy, either. It is a deviation from our dreams as a free people.*

We have here a realistic analysis that makes devils of no one, and which acknowledges the great gains and values of modern industrial civilizations. And while disclosing elements of great promise, some life-renewing expectations of our culture, it also discloses threats that involve all social groups alike, and may very well be at the root of our sense of helpless frustration. It is out of some such analysis, which suggests goals for our efforts, that we may learn to dream creatively again.

There are some for whom the American dream of a world politically free, free from superstition, tyranny, want, and violence is still a formidable and productive motivation, and they are desperately trying to recapture the vision of a better society. But I suspect these are the few. With many, instead of the projection of their best hopes in social outlook, we find projections of fear. As we read Orwell's *1984* or Nevil Shute's *On the Beach* and similar visions of doom, we realize that this nightmare is partly determined within us, and is at times housed in our souls to the enfeeblement of our beatific vision. I think it very wholesome to read such expressions of fear if we accompany them with study of such efforts as Frankel's so as to locate the undigested substances in our culture that have disturbed our dreaming. I am sure that, if we do this, we shall find that they are not as elemental as Scrooge's blot of mustard or bit of underdone potato. Such effort on our part is the first step in the reformation of our cultural purposes. Can the power-making agencies that do not ask for our consent be identified? Can they be taken out of the realm of anonymity? Can those who wield such powers be induced to accept and share social responsibility without curtailing our traditional freedom? That is our challenge. So our first task, as responsible citizens, is a very serious studiousness as a prelude to the reformulation of our faith—to the end that our faith and ideals may command our loyalties. Our religion should enable us to believe in the possibility of a warless world without feeling like naive fools. It should enable us to believe in a world to be, in which people are politically free without feeling that we are indulging in vain hopes wedded to an outmoded ideology that at best is merely romantically beautiful. We should have religion that would make it possible for us to protest the pollution of the air we breathe and our food and drink without being suspected of being in league with the "commies"; to raise voices against war without being suspected of disloyalty.

John Dewey used to disparage preoccupation with distant and generalized goals, and to emphasize the relatively higher value of the near, immediate, and realizable goals. He was very wise, for it is extremely easy for us to remain enamored of goals long after they have lost their significance for our really active purposing. But I accept the distant goal, or I should say the distant projection of our values, because it gives clues as to how to realize the near ones, or even to set them up. It is characteristic of man in his most creative moods. I doubt if even John Dewey could have explained why he always found democratic solutions for social problems except in terms of long-range projections of his operating values. Our values need to be housed in faith if we are not to be deprived of them.

We are long past the time when our moral responsibility is discharged by condemning robber barons, or hidden persuaders and waste makers. Our democratic political and industrial institutions have produced more for us than any social efforts ever have for any people. I can be personal here. If it had not been for scientific and industrial and legislative advances, I could not have pursued my particular vocation without contemplating the poorhouse or suicide upon reaching the age of retirement. It's still a narrow squeak, but not at all tragic.

Nevertheless, I cannot conceive of anything more moronic than the contention that we have a faultless society, and that all we need is to defend it against outlanders and barbarians. In a recent Christmas-time editorial in a college town paper I happen to know, the baby Jesus—the Prince of Peace—was with pious thankfulness associated with our military might, our supposed successful encirclement of our enemies, and our general preparedness for war. This easy acceptance of all we are and its association with our sacred hopes is not confined to small towns and innocents. I have read worse statements from more auspicious sources, and I know that there is a nucleus of a cult that makes a religion of the notion that we need no law or government that free industrial enterprise can't provide. The fact is that wherever there are significant advances new problems also emerge; the unanticipated developments always come forth as real threats; and if no one notes the new realities, the human dreams and the realities part company. Along with the feeling that all is not well, the nightmares begin. When we become merely defensive, merely holding to that we have and are, there is no longer any faith or dream to transmute troubles to creative hopes.

This is as true of business as it is of cultures. And I would add that effective defense against outlanders is contingent upon the knowledge of and successful conquest of our own spiritual weaknesses.

James Warburg, in his book *The West in Crisis,* calls the United States "the status quo power in a rapidly changing world." If this is true, and Warburg is no fool, it may go far in developing and explaining the relative success of the lying pretensions of the Soviet leaders. Those who don't know what is threatening them are wide open to deception, and can accept direction only from those who know what they are doing.

It is my conviction that the American Dream will regain its potency when it finds expression again in terms that catch up the realities of the present time, and when it finds expression in behalf of all peoples, when the theater of the Dream is not just America, but the planet. This amounts to saying, "when its spirit gives birth to a fresh and real dream." The pains and frustrations and hopes of Africans, and Asiatics, as well as of our own minority groups, must also be ours. It is no longer possible to invite the poor, the homeless, and tempest-tossed to hospitable shores. Even if we had room for them it would no longer do. We now live in one world-wide house of life and the faith and trust and mutuality that belong to a home have to be created. We have no other choice. We have power, unharnessed as it may be, in our honest concerns for the future of man, and we must learn to use it. But how? I have been close to several typical groups in our churches on this general problem, and I know of their shyness in witnessing to their values publicly, of their honest befuddlement over where to start and what to do. I must say something from their perspective, and that will not be difficult, for I am one of them.

CHAPTER 8

The Problem of Corporate Goodness

Fulfillment through participation in the reduction of the world's ills may be a good prescription, but a difficult one to have filled. Dreams are healthy when they can become realizable objectives. When society is viewed from the perspective of one who wishes to be creatively involved in it, it has a face as inscrutable as the face of "God," and as threatening to one's peace. Maybe this face too is the face of God if we view it as one of the phenomena of the Milky Way. If we cannot make such an identification we'll have to dig up the devil again. How useful "Auld Clooty" was! He didn't make doing good much easier, but he did make people feel less befuddled.

In the old days, being mindful of one's neighbor was a natural communal affair, almost an economic necessity. I remember my father undertaking the building of a barn. In the evenings after work hours he hewed timbers and cut and bored them to measure, made pins to join them, etc., until the whole structure was laid out on the ground. Then, when he gave the call, all neighbors within several miles came and together they erected the frame and boarded enough of it in to give it stability in a single day. What one couldn't do for oneself was done by the community, in what was called a "frolic," which was a work party with frolicsome touches. I remember, too, a widow who lived two farms away, and how every year her fields were plowed, seed sown, and harvest gathered in this way, and I never heard her spoken of as a burden. She had her own skills which she lavishly gave in return without even the necessity of a verbal contract. No neighbor was altogether independent. On the other hand there were no charitable institutions. The homes absorbed the unfortunates, even the insane except in violent cases.

In our day, your next-door neighbors don't seem to need you. They'd be ashamed to admit it if they did, at any rate. The one who does need you may be several thousand miles away, perhaps in Indo-China. There is no chance for a personal contact, but there are many agencies and instrumentalities of service between you and him. The good that you do is impersonal, often anonymous. The beneficiary of your good deeds may be grateful to an abstraction called America—that is, if he ever knows where his help came from.

A great many people find ethical achievement in serving the unfortunates nearer home who may be at times equally anonymous. So much of the good in the world, like so much of the evil, falls into this category of anonymity. The poor and distressed are always with us—crippled children, bedridden sick people, lonely and destitute old folks, those deprived economically who need all sorts of material assistance. But they do not need to be far away to be as anonymous as if in Indo-China. Many of these needs can be met in part with money. In fact, we are inclined to believe that money will care for them all. So we devise ingenious ways to make money for such purposes. There are, of course, those who add the personal touch, but they are few, and their charges never become neighbors in the old sense. We are, for the most part, conscious of physical needs, and American can be generous, even lavish, in response to such needs. Someone said in my hearing once that if anyone in America should undertake to organize an association for the relief of roasting peanuts, one could probably have a measure of success.

An issue of *Life*[1] gives an interesting perspective on the American way of doing good. There is a featuring of the old-fashioned neighborly way in communities with few enough people to make that way possible, where "a pinch of providence, a dollop of straightforward kindness, and a lot of plain hard work" will do what needs to be done. The ills of most of the world's unfortunate are, however, very far-flung and very complex. Doing good is no longer a matter of dropping in with a stew or an apple pie for a family in trouble. The need is massive, representing many millions of dollars and as many people. One of America's answers to this need is a blizzard of charity balls such as those which sweep New York City and many other places annually. The article says, "If it's a disease we have a ball for it. The impeccably dedicated Imperial Ball is given for hospitalized veterans, but whatever the cause, charity balls are fabulously lavish, increasingly commercialized, and startlingly similar—so much so that bored spouses are often heard loudly demanding, 'What the hell is this one for?'" In this convenient way of doing good, charitable impulses are mixed up with the display of pretty gowns, the desire to be photographed and publicly numbered among the smarter set, and incidentally, with the lure of sumptuous food and drink. It is easy to poke deprecating fun at this sort of thing, but when one faces the fact that these balls yield as much as forty-five million dollars yearly in New York alone, one is impressed despite the fact that the cost runs into the hundreds of thousands. We just have to salute and say, "Well done thou good and faithful league of the social register." After all, when one has the chance to overeat or get high, and feed the starving at the same time, let one go to it. It's not every day one can have one's cake and eat it, too.

And if people who do not give to causes in any other way are so induced to contribute to the general good, it's all the better. I am sure that Americans prefer this sort of thing—from the small town raffled quilt to New York's Imperial Ball—to being taxed. Probably this can be regarded as the lowest form of mutuality, that is, in terms of character involvement, but in institutional terms it is enormously important. It means food, shelter, clothing, and existence itself, to thousands.

There are other massive methods. Every organ in my body has a national association to stand guard over its health, at least to raise money for this purpose. Agencies to raise money for institutions have become institutions themselves, demanding other agencies and personal loyalties to serve them. Personally, I have never been able to find out what percentage of the money I give to any of the associations ever is used for the much advertised research. So I give with a certain amount of uncertainty and doubt.

I could easily be boring by adding to this list of massive aid by mentioning the billions of dollars our nation spends in many parts of the world to keep people eating and alive, or such things as the hundreds of millions of dollars spent annually by industrialists on higher education. At no point is American generosity better exemplified, and in many cases it does represent generosity and public concern. I am sure that among the donors are many, too, who contribute not out of compassion so much as to dodge taxes. In the last fifteen years charitable foundations have sprouted all over the country like mushrooms after a rain, and I am sure they haven't all come out of an upsurge of concern for the good of society. Yet the giver is no less important even if his motives be mixed. Without this effort our higher education would collapse and many of the best brains of the nation would go uncultivated.

Despite these many devices, and in part because of them, doing good has become extremely problematic. I can't even help my wife do the dishes; a machine does them, and I probably suffer a consequent decline in thoughtfulness. My next-door neighbors are so mostly in geographic terms. They really don't know whether I am alive or dead most of the time. The ideal is for each one of us to look after one's own needs. One's hope is that his insurance will cover all eventualities. If a person slips on a banana peel, on one's sidewalk, the policy cares for it and everything is all right. If the boy who puts up the storm windows breaks his neck, the insurance company compensates his family, and we are so glad we had the requisite foresight. If I haven't made provision for such eventualities, it's just too bad for me. I can be taken to the cleaners. And, for many, insurance even cares for conscience. But should it? This is an instance of Frankel's concern for our social texture. But if my children are left alone and dependent by death, the agencies will pick them up, and this is not quite so happy an arrangement in a home-loving country. But it is regarded as a retribution for failure. The ideal of our society is for each one to be sufficient unto oneself, from the time one matures until the end. The other day I made sensible arrangements for the disposal of my remains at the lowest possible price—and that could be regarded as the happy realization of a Scotsman's dream.

It's a new world, And it is a world in which we must operate ethically and not merely as individuals. We must create corporate agencies to represent us as well as to be personally and effectively responsible. And I am sure that we are emotionally as well as rationally unprepared for the great massive relations of modern times.

As a member of corporate society, I feel inadequate. Like the Wizard of Oz who was a very good man and a very bad wizard, I may be a very good man, but a very ineffective citizen. Someone, for instance, writes me that so and so is being railroaded to the electric chair by malign social forces, or is threatened with deportation. I hve no way to judge of his guilt or innocence, and I may do harm by giving, and I may do a great wrong by withholding.

Many unpopular causes call for support, for personal witnessing. What do I do? I have little or no contact with the community leadership. Shall I go into the streets and shout my protest? Join the beatniks and wave banners and so on? Such a necessity frightens people like me, and we are legion, and evil is probably thus entrenched in our timidity and fear. I may venture to do something towards giving a Communist a fair trial and I am branded and lose my job and so earn destitution for my family. Is this good? Wes Lawrence, a columnist with the *Cleveland Plain Dealer,* gave some interesting illustrations of this sort of dilemma in his column some time ago. The government sold at auction an Amish man's horses to pay the social security taxes he, on religious grounds, refused to pay. So the man has been deprived of his means of livelihood in order to provide him with security in his old age which he can never get because his religion will not permit him to accept it, but which he would have provided for himself if he had been left his means of making a living. In this whole project, too, one wonders if America really believes in freedom of religion. Lawrence works up several similar dilemmas with reference to issues such as the Freedom Riders, the exchange of Cuban prisoners for American tractors, and so on. We could suggest even more serious ones. What of feeding the hungry of the world in the face of the population explosion? What of the burden of old people on society as the result of advances in medicine and social legislation? So making up one's mind on how to address oneself to the critical situations with which our time and culture are faced can become nightmarish. For the people who don't care, who are not possessed of the values that create concern, all this confusion is an easy out. "It's all screwy, so forget it." But I believe that a tremendous number of Americans, and probably most of us, are deeply concerned, and wish very much to come to grips effectively with the ethical problems of our time. Being so motivated and so stymied by the complexity of doing good, many of us are unhappy.

What I have said on this puzzle represents pretty well the thoughts of the local church people with whom I have, in various groups, discussed this problem. In our discussions we gained insights, and some of us, probably, a change of feeling about the whole thing, but generally speaking, this is a problem that requires more than discussion. These people felt the frustration as keenly as I. They say they are not the sort to go out to join protest marchers, or to get into picket lines as we used to do in the twenties. They like to be effective in a legal, orderly, acceptable way. Anyway, what indications are there of good results from tearing one's hair in public? Evil and good get mixed up, too. You make a move to help an underprivileged person in the matter of housing and you bring unhappiness and maybe economic disaster upon neighbors whose respect and good will one needs and covets. On the other hand, when all possibilities are nicely calculated and you are determined to do good without embarrassing anyone, especially yourself, you become ethically and civically paralyzed at the very point at which the major social changes are taking place, and at which one's efforts are most needed. So runs the argument, and this is the dilemma of many.

Some people will go to great extremes to avoid unpleasantness. The *Saturday Review* quotes one such who declared that he would not have anything to do with the bomb shelter issue. He just left it alone, he said. At this point he noticed that he was talking to a lawyer, so he added: "Oh, you're a lawyer. How can I get a revolver permit? I want to be able to shoot myself and my family if we do have an atomic attack." It's a problem, all right.

I would like at this point to be able to suggest some way, or ways, out of the dilemma that would not embarrass anyone. Unfortunately, I haven't come up with anything but the conviction that such a way just can't be found. We haven't even the outlet of the fundamentalist who, after showing how unescapably worthy of damnation one is, can still refer people to the grace of God. As I heard one of these admit once, "I don't know how or why God would bother with such people, but God does." Yet I do not feel altogether helpless at all, and in this I have been greatly helped by discussion. And I *can* make suggestions.

I would say, first, that religion can be a real asset to us in seeing ourselves in the light of a new realism that the times call for. For example, I am afraid that I too am among the comfortable who have always faced the threat of spiritual degeneracy. Despite my dubious economic security, I never had it so good, and relatively few have. If all the people were as comfortable as I the millennium would be here! Some might say, "So why should you worry?" I remember a fellow soldier once inexpertly mouthing the inscription on the great British seal and then freely translating, "To hell with you Jack, I'm all right." If we felt that way we would not have any problem, but we don't feel that way. Our natures and culture call us to greater degrees of ethical and spiritual fulfillment than we seem able to achieve, and in addition, our tradition points a finger at the unconcerned. So we face the fear of embarrassment, of losing something, some comforts, and/or a bit of respectability in certain circles. We are in danger of becoming like the class Confucius hated so much— those who were comfortable and respectable and *gave every appearance of virtue,* yet were so identified with the conventions that not even a moral crisis could flush them from the protective coloring of their hideouts.

I at times work at the task of getting a different, a truer, image of myself, and I would recommend the effort. Can I be wrong in having the notion that I am a decent sort of chap, a likeable sort, one who would die to save his fellows at times maybe, reasonably responsive and generous in meeting human needs, a guy with certain professional achievements behind him, not altogether undeserving of a "well done thou good and faithful one." The therapists tell us that we should love ourselves. Well, I have gotten far enough in this loving oneself to know that there is something fishy about that image, and I don't want to love anything phoney. I feel heroic enough at times to give up, imaginatively, everything for a cause, but I rarely if ever get into a situation that is even slightly threatening. The crises have a way of flowing around me in all sorts of swirls and leaving me, for the most part, serenely alone. Have you, whoever you are, ever felt that way? Or am I the only one? I have a very real fear at times that in the civic and world arenas my goodness is far too often merely ritualistic. Eric Fromm through his recent book has made me very conscious of this possibility. I do believe in man, I respect every soul. I believe everyone should have food and education, and I have my beatific visions of things that should be, but what does my behavior spell out in these terms? It is in the mere liturgical fulfilment of good notions that the devil has throughout history gotten around *good* people. Nations always fall for it—"In God we trust," and that sort of thing. So I say, when we love ourselves let us do so to the degree at which we are no longer afraid to look at our limitations, and can look at them realistically as part of our condition.

Secondly, I think that we should also do something about the image we have of the corporate entity we call the church. Getting liberals of our tradition to work together is, at times, like eating peas with a knife. They come one by one, maybe. In accord with this tradition they say that we cannot really represent each other. We act as individuals, but corporately no. So the church is often spoken of as something that doesn't stand for anything but our individual rights to stand for what we please. Some suspect that even as individuals we find no command in our faith, just a privilege. Yet there is no denomination in which pulpits speak more of what the faith means, and none whose people are more effectively involved in civic affairs. But aside from this contradiction, the fact is that a corporation such as a church has character, inescapably so. It cannot be neutral. Despite the weight of feeling on this matter among us, if the church cannot operate as our agent of good, cannot be committed in any way, how can we expect our nation to have moral concerns and act ethically? How can it have moral significance and character? A sense of certainty often deserts me, but it doesn't at this point. The church cannot be less significant ethically as a corporate unit than its individual members are supposed to be. I am not alone in this feeling. Sermons often come to the desks of ministers from all over the denomination. Recently there has been a marked increase in the frequency with which they deal anxiously with this problem. They call attention to what one calls our "schizophrenia" and what another talks of as the "Tyranny of Freedom" that leaves people unchallenged and inert.

As I said to a church group during a discussion of the minority group housing problem, I believe that a church should, as a minimum effort, study its immediate environment and the social problems that are especially characteristic of the neighborhood, and the governing board should determine democratically how to deal with them. If it is a problem of housing for a member of a minority group the church should have seen the problem coming, if nothing more, and be ready to deal with it in a way that will not double-cross the very intent that brought its people together. Some churches are panicked by the sudden raising of such a problem. Fortunately, many are not. A number of churches are prepared. A Cleveland minister said to me not long ago, "When it comes to a real practical civic issue involving the right of people as humans I can fully rely on ninety-five per cent of my people." When this is so, the world about such a church knows about it, people are happier together, and even the church school teacher finds his or her job easier. I am sure that there are such churches who still will not act as corporate units. What a waste of spiritual power and of witnessing to the values we serve! But a church that has been indifferent and gets caught in an embarrassing crisis to its discredit, by the disclosure of what it actually is, is experiencing one of God's minor retributions.

A third thing I would say is that we cannot afford to excuse vulnerability in the presence of the disapproving neighbor, the disapproving community majority, or the big boss. I am also sure that we are often frightened by bogies of our own creation. I remember long ago sitting in a conference served by the Quaker Clarence Pickets and other leaders. Pickets made a certain suggestion for effective social action, and a lady in the group almost screamed, "But we'd be jailed for that!" His reply was, in effect, "Suppose we are. Some of us have been there before." I felt strongly that even going to jail was to this man one of the routine consequences of doing good and being true to himself and his faith, something that didn't occasion the stirring of either fear or heroics of any sort. We are so often so scared that we cannot think of action except in heroic terms and these frighten us even more. But the point I wish to make is that *when this good man could take it that way he suffered no indignity whatsoever, either in his own eyes or that of others.* And could this be true of any kind of unhappy consequence we anticipate? As the Cowardly Lion found out about his timidity, we're helpless largely because we think we are and, like the lion, we have a lot more to back up a little courage than most.

But difficulties will remain. A good attitude will not altogether remove mountains, but coupled with a little imagination it can go a long way.

I recently read an account of a police raid in New York City on a place that was suspected of harboring dope addicts. The place was filled by human derelicts who were being fed and bedded there. Among them were found some with dope and needles and they were arrested. The police also took along the seedy-looking proprietor as a promising suspect. He protested that he was not an addict, and furthermore said that he was not destitute, that in fact he was well off. Checking, they found that indeed he was not an addict, and that he was not only well off, he was a millionaire by name of John Cram. He was a modest chap. He felt that perhaps he was not doing a great deal of good, but he was sure that he was not doing any harm. When in court, the unfortunate immigrants of the area shouted in his behalf, calling him "Papa Dio," which suggests that perhaps he accomplished more than he supposed. What I like about Cram, assuming the correctness of the report, is his imaginative freedom, and the fact that he dispensed a human touch that few think of prescribing in such city areas. Moreover, he symbolizes something in our civilization that really mixes up our feelings.

There's a fourth thing that I can say in the face of the unnerving magnitude of modern problems. To expect opportunities for service to humanity to open up, and to be so clearly uninvolved in contradictions that what we will do will make everyone happy is a delusion born of weakness.

Perhaps the assistance of good causes by mail comes as close to getting involved without serious consequences as anything can. Norman Cousins says that if we just supported the good proposals and courageous efforts, we would have an incalculable effect on our national policy. He says this is the method used most effectively by extreme right wing, reactionary groups. But even this can be embarrassing to some. It may mean standing out of the crowd with one's convictions. It may mean being counted. But we cannot go anywhere without committing ourselves.

If I may tell a Scottish story: Sandy and Donald were clinging to some flotsam from their ship which had foundered in a gale. As night came on they were alarmed enough to try praying for help. Donald wasn't accustomed to praying much, but when he got going he did very well. He implored the Lord and began a long list of promises of good behavior should the Lord spare them, but when he was about to forswear strong drink for the rest of his life, Sandy grabbed him by the shoulder and shook him, saying, "Donald, Donald, dinna commit yoursel'! I see a licht." But I doubt if we are dealing with a situation in which we can dispense with assistance. Commit ourselves we must.

The obstacle is often just our fear. People who know and work with strong political leaders declare that such leaders are highly approachable and do respond to reason and unthreatening persuasion. I remember Lincoln Steffens long ago telling of a hard-bitten industrialist who was said to be ruthless with his workers and generally feared and hated. Instead of making angry speeches about him he went to see him and asked him why he didn't do thus and so. The reply was that that was a very good idea and that he would see to it, which he did.

Agencies such as the League of Women Voters, the NAACP, and others have found a number of effective ways. Many of them are reasonably and quietly effective, but these do not make the headlines. At times, challenge and the power of public opinion are required, and some agencies apply it, and I personally feel that this has to be done whether we like it or not, if we and America are to keep our souls.

But when every avenue is used, and every reasonable, quiet, and polite method employed, there will still be times and circumstances in which we can only protest. Protest has its civic function just as my conscience has a function. Even if the peace parade is the only thing that offers itself I'd kind of like to be in on it. I confess a certain jealousy for people like Roger Baldwin and Martin Luther King for their nights in jail. As for the peace parade, the beatniks will be there and the screwballs, but so will be people like Dr. Spock, who says that his interest in the welfare of children must be for all children, including those of tomorrow.

68

CHAPTER 9

Worship: The God-Human Relationship

When I first became a student in theological seminary I used to listen to seniors who served local churches discussing their preaching problems, and one thing I noted was that when a fellow had not prepared, or, for any reason, had nothing to say, he preached on worship or prayer. This was a theme on which he could get away with any nonsense, for it was the sacred cow of themes which no one dared desecrate with protest or question.

I wish to limit the theme slightly and ask, "What Can Worship Mean to Liberals?" Most of us cherish the God concept poetically, if at all, and that may be the best way to cherish it, but it does create difficulties with worship for people who have discarded so much of the tradition closest to them. There is among us a widespread disbelief in prayers of petition, of intercession, confession, etc., and often in any kind of prayer. Many, too, who believe in worship values are irritated to death by the old concepts and language that find their way into our worship services.

But this uncertainty and negation are far from being the whole story with us. We have a massive support from people for the typical church service as well as for private worship. I doubt that our churches would long survive without worship services. We have a strong feeling for worship and some real negative feelings, and, I suspect, without adequate rationale for either.

I remember back in 1928, when I was fresh from graduate study and just discovering liberals, I attended my first convention of Universalists. I was asked to speak on the educational values of the convention program. I naively indcluded their worshipping in my analysis, and asked why they had so many services. They began each day's deliberations with a king-sized one, and most every session with at least some advisory suggestions to the Almighty—which reminds me of a prayer I love that is supposed to have been made by some devout deacon. He said, "Use me, dear Lord, in thy work, especially in an advisory capacity." But I'll get back to the convention—I asked sincerely if they had asked themselves what values were to be thus derived for themselves or others, and expressed the desire to be enlightened on the psychological and/or spiritual or educational process involved that might lead to better programming and control. They assumed I was against worship because I suggested thinking about it. A lady preacher rose with heaving bosom and declared, "I am *for* worship." Thus the first shot was fired in a battle that made me shy of ever mentioning the subject again.

Nevertheless, I firmly believe that worship involves an inescapable kind of response to life on the part of man and woman, and that that something is of some real consequence to the individual and civilization alike.

We may think of worship as the internal activity of the religious spirit. (I first wrote that as "infernal activity," but despite Freud I blame the typewriter.) Worship is charged with feeling and with thought, but it isn't merely thinking about life. It is rather the hot focus of living in which human needs and desires contend with life's demands, limitations, and conflicts. If this be true, worship should mean a great deal to liberals—as much as to anyone else. The reason for worship is the reason for any religion at all. The evolutionary venture of becoming human costs us something. We aren't on any gravy train or joy ride as we seek an adequate sense of being.

A human being is a conflict ridden organism. Each has the longings and needs of immortals, but are as finite as any creature. The tension resulting between these poles is the source of religion, and of much of one's creativity generally, and possibly of destructiveness too. The novelist Faulkner said, in his Nobel Prize speech, that the problems of the human heart in conflict with itself were the only things worth writing about, worth the sweat and agony involved. And I add that a man or a woman has to settle with the fact that each is as expendable as the worm on its leaf, and must make his or her peace with death or go down fighting. But there is more than

70

this involved. A human being's nature is not only divided against itself; this being is only partially conscious of what one is. One may identify oneself with civilizing values and still be potentially destructive and bestial. One has to deal with what has been called the demonic in oneself or what we today call the unconscious, with all its dark motives and urges. Let me quote from Carl Jung's *The Undiscovered Self.*

Since it is universally believed that man is merely what his consciousness knows of itself, he regards himself as harmless, and so adds stupidity to iniquity. He does not deny that terrible things have happened and still go on happening, but it is always "the others" who do them. . . . Man has done these things; I am a man who has his share of human nature; therefore, I am guilty with the rest, and bear unaltered and indelibly within me the capacity and the inclination to do them again at any time. Even if, juristically speaking, we are not accessories to crime we are always, thanks to human nature, potential criminals. In reality, we merely lack a suitable opportunity to be drawn into the infernal melee. None of us stands outside humanity's black collective shadow . . . one would therefore do well to possess some 'imagination in evil' for only the fool can permanently neglect the conditions of his own nature. In fact, this negligence is the best means of making him an instrument of evil. Harmlessness and naiveté are as little helpful as it would be for a cholera patient and those in his vicinity to remain unconscious of the contagiousness of the disease.[1]

Strong words, these, yet not so much stronger than those from other analysts. When you read them you may also hear John Knox, or a contemporary of his, thundering about the devil incarnate.

Humankind has peopled heaven and earth with Gods and devils in conflict, with spirits, jinns and hobgoblins, Heaven and Hell. We have conceived of an eternal war between light and darkness and so on. And we have done this in all probability because such forces reside within ourselves. Whenever I read the great analysts I get the feeling that giving up the devil was a great mistake. But whatever the realities of our soul's turmoil may be, we have to take ourselves seriously. The inner war was known long, long before Freud and his successors. How well the early Christians knew of it, and so with others, centuries before they appeared.

Carl Jung worries a great deal over the loss of myth and symbol in Western culture, for he thinks these served to release and control the unconscious. We may not need to pin such faith on myth and symbol. Perhaps we are tough enough to confront what he calls "The Shadow" directly, but we can only take human nature lightly at our peril. And no one who takes him or herself seriously as a being in a civilization of beings can easily escape being a worshipper. It is very unfortunate that this great function has gotten identified with particular expressions of it. Our worshipping tendency always stands in judgment of any particular worship form.

I don't know how to communicate what I feel sure about in other than pesonal terms, which is probably not good form. But I must say that there are many ways in which I take myself seriously. It isn't just a matter of, in a sophisticated way, going fishing now and then in the sea of Id, as Arthur Foote says, to see what curiosities we can bring up—worship is not a hobby. I don't say prayers except publicly in church (and please don't jump to any conclusions about that), yet I think I worship a great deal. I even think I know what the old-time religionists meant by "praying without ceasing." I may be reading an article in the *Saturday Review,* or maybe a newspaper, or one of the Greek or Shakespearean tragedies, or even a "who-dunnit," and I am suddenly arrested by a challenge to some of my unfounded assumptions, to my pet prejudices and certainties, or to my irresponsible vacillations, pretenses and self-deceptions, and I have to make corrections in thought and behavior. It may be, too, that I am made aware of the deeply rooted destructiveness that is dormant within me. Being a member of the Fellowship of Reconciliation and discovering myself experiencing impatience with Hamlet because he did not at once dispatch the king when he was at his prayers is a deeply revealing experience. It may be, on the other hand, that my sense of dedication and convictions and values are confirmed and enhanced, and I feel very good indeed. It may be that I am so overwhelmed by the beauty with which a truth is stated or lived that I am speechless with wonder and gratitude.

Just as much can happen, too, when I converse with persons, or work with them. The truth can hit like lightning when I am mowing the lawn, or stirring the oatmeal in the morning. Sometimes I am moved with wonder like a child, with something I cannot match in word or thought. Sometimes I am too crushed by the enormity of the problematic. Sometimes I just have to learn to take what life does to me. What all this does to one's conception of the self is no little matter, for it is definitely related to such creative powers as I have, and certainly to one's capacity for understanding and for compassion for those who break under life's tensions.

Worship has been described in many ways, but always the descriptions contain this matter of knowing one's inner nature, releasing and controlling it. We can think of it as living in a tremendously inclusive context, involving the universe, our value goals, life's frustrations, along with the expectation that assistance will come to us—will, wisdom, or courage—to do what must be done. I doubt if the analysts ever invented anything better in the way of preventive therapy than a Quaker meeting, with, of course, the Quaker's faith and expectations. It is worth remembering that Freud and Jung and other greats in analysis borrowed something for their therapy from the confessional. It is very difficult to convince people of all this. But one who has learned to respect all life, as such, knows what I mean. One who has learned to love all sorts and conditions of people knows. One who has learned to face death with serenity knows. Worship hallows all life and empowers the spirit of the worshipper. It begins in our needs and our feelings; it may end in fresh thought and understanding, in resolve and dedication, or in serenity and happiness.

Jacob Trapp says that worship first arose in a creature who had the capacity for thought and only in such a creature, and that is a thought for those who bracket worship with primitive behavior patterns.

I am sure all this is not too strange to many of us. Worship belongs to life. You'll find it, or it will find you, between the stove and the sink, between the home and the office, while buying and selling (and I wish it happened oftener here), in acts of hiring and firing, in play and gaiety, in the faces of children, in the faces of sufferers and old folks, and in the eloquent faces of the indifferent and unconcerned, and the innocently unaware—anyone. It comes happily, too, with a "well done" for something accomplished, comes in the delights of form and sound and movement and texture, etc., either from the hand of the artist or from nature itself. As someone has said, worship is not so much talking to God as it is God talking with you. (This recollection is probably also from Jacob Trapp, who writes eloquently on the inner life.)[2] Its reality is witnessed, too, by the fact that, as James Martineau says, you know a person by what he worships, for which he yearns, be it money, vengeance, or the capacity to love. What we ask of life suggests its direction, and how its energies are used up. In a mature faith worship has to do with long-range values and hopes as they play on our internal and outward circumstances. There is orientation of attention toward all that matters most. It has to do with the inner ordering of life and its discipline.

I am sure I have stirred some impatience by now. "You're talking about things everyone experiences and we never thought of as worship. And what about corporate worship? Why do we need a church? Why do we have to come here and sing hymns with outlandish theology? Why not leave worship in life, if that's where it is?" I have much sympathy with such inquiries. Until recently I used to think that only twice in my life had I gotten values from church, and I acknowledged that those two occasions were significant enough to make up for all the times I came away from church with empty head and heart.

But lately I have come to know that the church was much more involved in my personal and out-of-church experiences of devotion than I had supposed. A very important factor was that the church was responsible for my system of values with which I worshipped anywhere, and for the first serious thinking I ever did. The long-range values were rooted in human experience, and not parochially derived, and the doctrines, outrageous as some of them seemed, addressed me to the issues of life. I feel corporate worship has made a great contribution to the preservation and dissemination of human experience—over the merely contemporary and the local. Yet I acknowledge that I often have gone home from church wondering why I hadn't gone fishing, or bird watching, or why I just didn't stay in bed. The fact is I did go fishing, now and then, to escape the intellectual and emotional poverty of a church, and I probably would have stayed in bed, too, if it were not for the fact that nothing but illness can keep me in bed in the morning. People have a right to make demands of public worship services. It is reasonable to demand that worship stir one's mind. I wish it to be addressed to my life and time, although I don't want it to be merely contemporary or to toady to my particular needs all the time. I require beauty of it, too, that ministering angel that so helps to make life tolerable.

The job of worship which I have suggested calls for mental activity—a feeling out for the truth, for dedication and beauty, and I think it also calls for a communal expression. It is no little matter that here we acknowledge by our presence that we share the hazards of life, and that life has to be taken seriously in common as well as individually. This is the only way in which many get the needed wide perspective on life, the leisure of sitting and thinking about it all. And there's another matter. Personally I never could get as much objectivity about myself, say, as a student and teacher of psychology, as I can in a church service that reaches me. The experience may have little to do with the sermon or anything else going on. I sometimes turn the sermon off and make good use of the time on my own. But I do something here that I do not do on the hillside or seashore. Perhaps the most significant thing about it is what I used to call "A God's-eye view of myself."

74

Public worship has too often been sinful in its shallowness and ugliness. The wonder is that it has persisted so. Heaven knows it needs to be improved in most places still. In the greater use of the arts, for instance. Music is closer to people than most arts, while at the same time it is one of the genius's greatest media of expression. But I would like to live long enough to see other art media used in the sanctuary with equal seriousness and skill. Why, for instance, shouldn't we watch a highly-skilled artist speak of life in the dance from a chancel instead of always listening to sermons? Closely associated with religion, along with the dance, was the drama, and I confess that good drama reaches me more deeply than sermons. One of my unforgettable religious experiences was in New York at a theater, watching Dudley Diggs and his associates doing a play on the theme of death. It destroyed for me forever the grim image of death that haunted my early life, and did so by the simple device of having death played by a smiling young man in a neat brown business suit, and by his matter-of-fact and kindly conversation with the dying.

It is unfortunately that, at the best, drama in churches is associated with special interest groups, and never takes the center of a service of worship, is never performed before the altar, even though that altar symbolizes the greatest of all dramas, that of life, death, and salvation. We should make a more representative use of art. The poet could tell us what he or she has seen in the face of God, or a reader with something of the skill of a Charles Laughton could represent God. It is not to the credit of our culture that the arts have been so removed from the sanctuary and cheapened by their commercialization—too bad, because their themes, the themes of music, drama, poetry, sculpture, etc., are also the concerns of the human soul in worship. In them is the stuff of worship, the difference being that the *worshipper* is the crucified one acquainted with grief, or the triumphant one; the worshipper is Macbeth, King Lear, Hamlet or St. Joan, or Job or Gideon, and goes to hell and back with Dante. Worship, personal or corporate, has been associated with every great faith and culture, whether these were God-centered or not. To dismiss such historic data as naiveté and ignorance in primitive man, particularly in the light of what analysis has confirmed about our natures, is probably as naive a notion as one can fancy. It isn't only the analysts who tell us of our real condition. It's some time since the Greek dramatists did it. It's some time since St. Paul despaired over the gulf between his good intentions and his behavior. And today every great voice speaks the truth for us: Hemingway,

Faulkner, Shaw, MacLeish, or Steinbeck. Can anyone read them without sensing the responsibility of taking life seriously, or ordering and directing the tumult of conflicting potentialities with which we were born?

And so, this is no "come to church" plea I am making. I am calling attention to the nature of life as explaining worship and requiring it. And I am making certain claims. I claim that when we think our own private ability or self-direction was inborn or due to one's superior intelligence, that it came without benefit of anyone's concern or prayers, one is being shallow-minded. I claim that a person who is not living superficially, and is not engrossed in escaping from life somehow or other, worships. I claim that public worship has a civilizing function, that it enables us to give us historic dimension to our meditations, and one of psychological depth, that comes only to the few in solitariness. And I will make this claim, and this is my last word: when we walk into a church to engage in worship, we may be doing the most significant thing human beings have ever done.

CHAPTER 10

Faith and Skepticism

H. L. Mencken is reported to have said that Unitarianism wasn't Christianity at all, but a kind of mattress for skeptical Christians to fall on. He should have known that there are skeptical stray sheep amongst us, too, from other than Christian folds. Lucky are all concerned that there is such a mattress. There is a notion abroad that Unitarian Universalists are unbelievers, and there is the notion, too, that skepticism belongs only with unbelief. Actually, skepticism has a very important place in the religious consciousness, as both psychology and history can show.

Says a character in the *J.B.* version of Job:

I know. I know. I know. I've seen him.
Job is everywhere we go,
His children dead, his work for nothing,
Counting his losses, scraping his boils,
Discussing himself with his friends and physicians,
Questioning everything—the times, the stars,
His own soul, God's providence.[1]

Of course Job gets censured for his doubts, but his story becomes a religious classic. So too with Gideon. While these men had no occasion in their time to doubt God's existence, they very much challenged God's wisdom and justice. So skepticism is associated with many of the great souls, and with the most deeply religious among them. To bring the matter up-to-date, let me read a bit from a currently popular theological work:

The passion for truth is silenced by answers which have the weight of undisputed authority, be it that of the mother or father or an old friend, or a gang, or the representatives of the social pattern. . . . The authorities gave him something to live on, the revolt makes him responsible for the truth he accepts or rejects. The revolt is as unavoidable as his early dependence. . . . Don't give in too quickly to those who want to alleviate your anxiety about truth. Don't be seduced into a truth which is not really your own, even if the seducer be your own church. . . .

This is Paul Tillich talking.[2]

We can say truthfully that skepticism is a facet of the gem of faith; that it quite naturally accompanies a great faith. Founders of religions had to lay aside cherished traditions because of some other things they believed—all of them that I can think of had to. The reformers, and many of the greats within a faith at any time, are, in more than one sense, deviants in conviction. The person who is concerned about the truth, who wants anything to say about what he believes, needs to use more than just an occasional pinch of salt.

The reason for this is probably in the fact that skepticism is as natural as sex, and just as difficult to eradicate. I need not say that the Cathari and the later Shakers, despite the admirable features of both these faiths, died out from unpopularity and lack of issue more than from persecution. The tenet of sexlessness was death to them. And skepticism cannot be more profitably eliminated than sex. The great religions have learned something of this, and in the hard way, and have found other than official ways to keep the sheep in the folds.

The skeptical impulse is self-assertive, self-realizing in function. It is pretty well established that there is a uniqueness in the individual religious sentiment. One must somehow make good the sovereignty of one's being or live the consequences of undeveloped gifts and stunted spiritual growth. This is probably why almost every child at one time or another comes up with a "no" to everything. He or she may not yet be able to back up the "no," but is serving notice that he or she has a soul that is no one else's.

Despite the evidence of this in human behavior since time immemorial, the exploratory activity of the individual mind has not been gently treated, and certainly not cultivated, by the authorities. One's self-asserting spirit was often regarded as devil-inspired, and it had to be broken. It became a grievous sin to be a deviant, to doubt the generally accepted truth. So heads fell, people were burned, tied to stakes where the tide would get them, or destroyed in many other ingenious ways, and to this day more subtle methods of coercion, less lethal but no less effective, are employed.

In John Bunyan's classic, *Pilgrim's Progress*, among the hazards on Christian's journey to the Celestial City were Doubting Castle and its proprietor, Giant Despair. Christian and his friend Hopeful were incarcerated in a black dungeon for days before Christian remembered that he had a key hidden in his shirt called "promise" that would open any door. So with this master of all master keys they went through doors, gates, and walls to freedom. Later on, Christiana and Great Heart also reached Doubting Castle. By this time Bunyan was really feeling his spiritual oats, and had Great Heart engage Giant Despair in mortal combat, and he cut off his head and demolished Doubting Castle.

So it seems doubt was taken rather seriously, even coupled with despair, and it has been regarded as a spiritual threat up to modern times. A good seminary professor of mine, a scholar of some eminence, and as individual as they come in many respects, wrote a successful book on the art of relieving doubt. Doubt was something to beat and abolish. It seems, however, that religion in such efforts asked too much of the human mind in the way of credulity and conformity. The Christian world view and scheme of salvation were probably deemed reasonable in the Judea of the first century. But not so to many outside that area, at first. It all seemed nonsense to many, and got more rather than less incredible as time went on, and so required more and more unquestioning faith. But all sorts of people broke with it one way or another, the most honest refusing to give it even lip service. The scientifically-minded Leonardo da Vinci was suspected of being the antichrist of his time. And, by the way, a reading of the trilogy of historical novels by Merethowski, *Leonardo da Vinci, Julian the Apostate,* and *Peter and Alexis,* suggests the great significance of the antichrist concept, and its association with the independent mind. Movements broke through such as the Renaissance, the Enlightenment, and finally the scientific revolution.

Of course ours is the heyday of skepticism. If one can write a thoroughly skeptical book in an informed, competent way, he is sure to have a best seller. And in our time, when so many shake off the power of authority, we need such books. Walter Kaufmann's *The Faith of a Heretic*[3] is a good example, a most useful book to those who have to make up their own minds, but disturbing to those who need authority. There are more drastic books. *The Future of Unbelief* by Gerhard Szczesny[4] is surely one of the most formidable attacks on Christianity in modern times, and it seems to have been taken most seriously by theologians in Europe where it first appeared. This author believes that the incredible Christian world view and scheme of salvation are believed by very few, but that the majority do not dare acknowledge their skepticism. Consequently, he thinks that this world view stands in the way of building a world view with faith and symbols that could be consistent with modern knowledge. He even has a chapter on "The Duty to be Unholy and Unwise." This book is not a skeptical treatment of Christianity by a rationalist who has no use for any thinking beyond the bounds of scientific knowledge. He believes that one has to reach beyond his grasp with philosophy, imagination, symbol, and myth, and he represents not the scorn of the narrow rationalist, but a passionate interest in destroying Christianity not merely because it is incredible, but because it obstructs the development of a healthy faith more in keeping with modern knowledge. Many things can be said in its favor, and it raises questions, too. For instance, it will not be easy to find a world view consistent with modern knowledge so long as modern knowledge is not too consistent with itself. Also, there's a lot more to Christianity than he mentions. He fights some straw men, and vaguely suggests a kind of straw salvation. Nevertheless, the book is a shaker of foundations, and good for those who have to nurture their own souls, and even for those responsible for the faith of others.

I have a bit of a guilty conscience about outlining this picture of skepticism as something rooted in nature as the ever-present friend of reason. I would correct the picture a bit by warning against identifying skepticism too much with high rationalism. I do not believe that humans are yet as rational as what I have said implies. I do feel certain that a human being wants and needs to protest and be skeptical, but I believe that he or she is thus so in order to select the objects of his or her own credulity at least as much as for the reason that he or she wants to get at the real truth. What I am suggesting is that we can be skeptical without being very rational. There is a nice distinction here, and a very important one. Protest can be as irrational as belief. I have known people who repudiated religion and church with all their works and yet fervently believed in astrology and flying saucers. I have just received an invitation to subscribe to a magazine that proposes to encourage such notions with articles from people of distinction—the truth of flying saucers, mind reading, and the relation of the galaxies to one's personal destiny. Such a magazine is a commentary on human credulity among the dissenters. What one wants more than one does truth is the right to believe or disbelieve anything.

Nevertheless, real rational skepticism accompanies great faith. No one can affirm any great faith without being skeptical of something else. No one could believe more in the infallibility of the Bible in matters of faith than Martin Luther. Yet he called the epistle of James "an epistle of straw." He did this because he believed in salvation by faith, and the author of the epistle seemed to stress good works as the way of salvation. So Luther concluded that James should not have been included in the canon. It's not so different with us. If one believes that God is love and is incapable of condemning and destroying the innocent, one will have trouble with hell and infant damnation as the Universalists did. If one believes that the universe is one natural order, one will have qualms about immortality and the supernatural. If one believes that nature is law-abiding, one will doubt the miracles, and so on. Liberal religionists are often regarded as negationists, and some deserve the label, but if even the extremists examined their negations they would find occasion for them in some other things that they do believe.

This all spells out the fact that skepticism is essential to thinking, a normal part of it, without which there could be no creative thought. When we find skepticism, so-called, without any attempt at constructive thought, we have something other than thinking.

I am sure that Unitarian Universalists do not need to be aided and abetted in skepticism, nor do they need to be convinced that skepticism is a good thing. What might make this statement relevant to them is that there are some (I think too many) who pride themselves on skepticism as an end in itself, who regard it as a personal virtue, and not as something involved in acts of serious discrimination. There are, of course, times when we must keep on saying "no" like a child to keep our souls even when we do not see a glimmer of the truth we need. This enlists my sympathy. But I am also sure that at times so-called skepticism serves as an escape from responsibility. One can fence oneself about in this way and live under the illusion that one is not being coerced by anyone or anything when one has simply given power to life's coercing forces by making them anonymous and unconscious. One can loudly disclaim belief in religion and church or causes or institutions that might seek one's support and so be responsible for nothing. The formulation of an article of faith for oneself is a highly responsible act. One can hardly claim in our day to be mature and educated and yet live without belief, without mental effort that even outreaches reason. It is very important that the imaginative reaches and beliefs and symbols we use be consistent with our experience as far as possible, but to claim independence of thought and not to reach out in thought is to live evasively.

We all know those who used their skeptical impulses to get out from under what they regarded as an intolerable theological inheritance, those who dismissed it as so much bunk, walked away from it, and instead of finding answers to life's questions for themselves ignored the whole business as unnecessary to one's existence. If such are lucky enough, preoccupied enough, or insensitive enough to experience, and they die early enough, they may get away with it. But the old life-and-death questions have a way of coming back, especially in maturity. Suddenly they are there, and if one has not sought answers there is nothing to turn to but the old repudiated doctrines. That is probably why some go back to the faiths of their childhood, or make a belated and frantic effort to find answers when they can no longer ignore their need.

There is no liberation without reinvolvement. This does not mean jumping from the frying pan into the fire. The reinvolvement can be our happiest bid for life fulfillment. The way to deal with a doubt is to go through with it when encountered. Julian Huxley says that he is too much of a skeptic not to believe that anything is possible. Add to this the feeling that most anything can be illusory, and one is at rock bottom where he must, and is free to, build again. Doubt honestly followed through can yield something constructive and positive, even though we must begin with the evaluation of humanity's guesses, and choose something from among humanity's illusions to live by.

I have found that in dealing with young people the only way to take their protests against "the faith of their fathers" is to help them carry through, rather than countering them and persuading them, until they begin to construct in harmony with what they know and feel. Treated thus they generally incorporate in their thought systems the great human values. To find their own sovereign sense of being is necessary to taking on the wisdom of humanity. This suggestion is as pertinent to Unitarian Universalists as to anyone. We encourage the natural revolt, and the fact that we have it in good measure is too little noted. Can some of our youth possibly repudiate our free faith? They can and they do.

Perhaps the prevailing fault of Unitarian Universalists is that they

82

have not done a fraction of what they could have done with their skepticism. They have demonstrated that very sensitive and religious people can be highly skeptical, and have thus brought together two things that were historically antithetical. They have shown, too, that they can enjoy a close fellowship while cultivating differing convictions. They have demonstrated that the agnostic and atheist can be religious, and that some of God's champions can be irreligious. But they have not followed out their skepticism in terms of programming and leadership, especially with adults. They still use the programming pattern of the little village church. In huge urban churches people lose contact with each other, except for an inner corps of workers. There is little exchange of thought, little mutual stimulation, little experience in making people at home with differences, no way of capitalizing on the skepticism and the creative efforts of the many. I have had great faith in the liberal venture of using differences creatively, and success has been demonstrated here and there, but I must confess to doubt at times. There is a real possibility that we too, like so many church groups, can stamp away in the same spot like soldiers drilling on a parade ground without going anywhere. Yet here is a focal point of a free faith, in the realm of skepticism, where we must find a certain sense of direction, and a more specific notion of our unique mission.

CHAPTER 11

Making the Most of What We Believe

How can we make the best of this theologizing, and/or philo-sophizing, that we insist on being privileged to do for ourselves? The privilege carries an imperative. If we do not seek our way we discredit the very idea, and if we seriously undertake to think out our own beliefs we should know something of what is involved, and something of the difficulties we are sure to encounter.

When one becomes aware of the values and assumptions by which one lives one may well find that one believes something more, or something much less, than one's unexamined life might suggest. Some people harbor strange beliefs that do them little credit as intellects, yet which may endear them to us. A university professor friend of mine, a man of gentle spirit and unquestioned scholarship, believed not only in immortality, which wasn't so strange, but also that his dogs and cars and other creatures he had loved would be with him in Heaven. This could have had little to do with his frontal lobe, but it *was* a measure of his love for all creatures, and maybe also of his great need to make his peace with life.

It is also true that a great many people get along with a few simply expressed ideas. and these may serve them better than elaborate philosophies may serve others. For a certain one it may be enough to believe in honesty, or that "God is love," or that the individual has a divine potential. One may invest such concepts with enough significance to make them serve a useful and dedicated life. In the days of my youth when a play on words was as attractive as the truth itself, I remember saying that the simple faith was the faith of a simpleton. I wouldn't be that simple now. But simplicity can be overdone. There was a soldier in my army unit who, although a Catholic, never went to mass or confession, but who did finger a medal hung about his neck and cross himself on awesome occasions, and tip his hat when passing a Catholic Church. This approaches being simple in the derogatory sense.

An Irish Catholic and an Englishman and my friend Sandy Mac-Tavish were once shipwrecked, and as they clung together to a broken spar and night came on, they were driven to desperate measures. They decided to try prayer. The Irishman couldn't produce anything that didn't sound like profanity, and the Episcopalian couldn't recall a single prayer, and so they both turned to Sandy, rather hopelessly I'm afraid, but Sandy at once responded with the suggestion, "Let's take up a collection!" But barring such naiveté, simplicity may represent a most successful capacity for life fulfillment.

There are people who seem to carry on a feud with life similar to that between the Martins and the McCoys, and a considerably larger number are hardly on speaking terms with life at all. Sometimes we all have such moods temporarily. I confess to feeling towards the Creator at times like my very young son once felt towards me in one of those less happy moments in a family when he defiantly asked, "Why did you borned me anyway?"

Nevertheless, we have a responsibility for thoughtfulness. Some are frightened by such responsibility, frightened of the empty reaches of the mind, and maybe of the great realities it discloses, and take refuge in an assumed lack of ability or of educational experience. But actually thoughtfulness is not dependent upon extraordinary endowment and erudition for maturity in thoughtful living. There are some unlettered woods guides and laborers who are more thoughtful than some erudite college professors. Some people are naturally more thoughtful than others, yet it is probable that most of us who are disinclined to think about life are not so much ungifted in concern and ability as we are nurtured in evasiveness. Even what we call tentativeness and "thinking for oneself" can be excellent hideouts. On the other hand, there are clear indications that a significant percentage of our people think very seriously. A man may pass around the cigars at the birth of his child with an air suggesting that he himself is the source of all life and had never given a thought to the wonder of how mother earth gave birth to life or whither his life tends. But know him better and you may find that he, too, has been peeking long and seriously over the rim of eternity.

Some worry more than they think. Others search among books and churches for a faith in which they can believe, like the itinerant true-gospel seekers of the Middle Ages, but personal responsibility cannot easily be evaded without a heavy price. In a church such as ours we have served notice on all and sundry that we don't take anyone's say-so as truth until we test it, and, ten to one, we don't take it then. So we are not the kind of people who should have to fumble and mumble when asked what we believe.

We should not be timid about our beliefs. We should have a good, confident feeling about them. They are a vital part of the self with which we cannot be at war in any sickly way. We have a right to our beliefs whatever they may be. Believing for oneself as a right should release the powers of one's belief. We should not be intimidated into silence about them by people or circumstances. I like these words from Albert Camus:

Nothing gives me the right to judge from above an epoch of which I am completely a part. I judge it from within, confusing myself with it. But I hold to the right of saying, henceforth, what I know about myself and others, only on the condition that this may not add to the unbearable misery of the world, but rather will indicate, in the dark walls against which we grope, the yet invisible places where the gates may open. Yes, I hold to the right of saying what I know, and I shall say it. [1]

As we dwell upon life's complexities, and are made daily wiser by experience, certain notions emerge that seem to become more and more unshakable, even when we know that they are not generally acceptable, or when we suspect that they are not too logical or reasonable. While granting every right to privacy, I think it unfortunate to be too shy of sharing the manner in which we keep our souls. Other souls need our insights for building their thought structures, even when they cannot accept them. But the need and right of expression are there apart from all consequences. One may harbor doubts of God and be afraid to admit to them, or one may cling to a faith in God in a company in which such faith is not too highly respected; yet growth in understanding comes more easily when we share our insights and concerns and gropings. I have met people who regard a request at a meeting for all to share their convictions as they might a request to appear undressed in public. There is something at work here which is not just the commendable sense of privacy. Anyway, exchange of observations and convictions about life is a stimulus to thoughtfulness, and quite indispensable to some people. One who wants to paint pictures, and must begin with something of no greater merit than a kindergarten product (and which may have limitations born of fear that are rarely found in kindergarten products), has to acknowledge this deformity as one's own offspring before one ever can exhibit anything that is more one's own that the instructor's, and before any of one's natural talents are available. So with beliefs. When genuine they are as individual as faces, and should be acknowledged.

A statement of faith does not merely demonstrate intellectual ability. It can be a measure of one's identification with life, or one's response to the universe, a measure of one's love for people, one's generosity of spirit and compassion or one's commendable protest. Among the realities a mind must deal with are one's own needs and one's own involuntary responses to the realities. To be rational about life, to get at the stark realities, is not the only concern. One has to find a way to live with the realities and befuddlements—we have to "watch in the dark walls against which we grope for the invisible places where the gates may open." If we judge thinking in these terms too, we will find people are often wiser than they know, and it is a pity that they should downrate themselves.

I would say also that a vital belief must reflect the stuff of one's life, and feed back direction, drive, and restraint to that life. It shows the assumptions and convictions about life's worth and limitations by which one lives. It is common for professed thoughts and ideals to have little or no connection with the lives of those who profess them, while such lives are governed by unexamined and unacknowledged, or highly compartmentalized, values and assumptions. Such thoughts are like the beautiful, moisture-laden clouds that float over parched earth for weeks without blessing it with a shower. Living one way and thinking another used to be called hypocrisy—a hard word that made it easier to identify the fault with some other fellow. In reality this is a very common tendency, afflicting all to a degree, no doubt, and especially nations and all corporate bodies, and it represents the oldest and cleverest method of self-deception ever devised. And there is nothing more destructive to mind or person or institution.

To say that one is not as good as one's professed ideals is not the same thing. One's reach should exceed one's grasp. This is natural and inevitable to some extent to anyone living within the context of great values. I refer rather to the thinking and professing that is outside the context of one's life. The more I live the more I am aware of the many ways we devise to cushion life's hard realities, and the less I am inclined to condemn or reprove anyone. But this device hides a person from himself or herself as well as from others, and one cannot be very permissive towards it. It is like some medicines with which I have had experience, which can help a disease yet kill the patient.

This may all be taken as a plea for genuineness. Our world is full of circumstances that tend to create despair as well as they do war and crime. The old moorings have given way to the floods of time and disaster. As a religious fellowship we have wilfully attempted what I believe to be somewhat unprecedented in history, namely, to get a new orientation in history, one not exclusively of the culture to which we were born. We feel that one tradition cannot fully serve us any more.

While retaining our sense of indebtedness to it we seek to sift other traditions in an effort to find or create a *human* tradition in the one world so suddenly thrust upon us. The seeking and thinking and prayerfulness this calls for should not permit anyone to take life lightly and thoughtlessly, however secure one may otherwise be. So I say that the first requisite of our address to the world in our time is genuineness. And genuineness means both awareness and honesty about life and ourselves. Without this, thinking for religious purposes is futile. Everything we do and encounter should make its contribution to our faith. As I said before, we may not accept the Bible claim that the sparrow's fall in God-noted, but there is cosmic as well as personal significance in the fact that *we* note it. I may say, "I believe in man rather than God." And when I come home bushed from work and offended and take my irritation out on my family, what relation has this behavior to my faith in humanity, and my understanding of it or to my faith in human morality? What does it suggest that I owe other peole in faith and understanding? One may have, for example, the responsibility of hiring and firing people. I was never a businessman, but more than once I have been faced with the necessity of recommending the release of employees whose need of employment was as acute as mine, and whose children were just as innocent and tender as mine. Isn't it important to know whether or not this worked itself into my philosophy of life and alerted me to such issues for my future and others' good? Tragedy hits a neighbor and we almost instinctively breathe a prayer of thankfulness that the angel of death passed over us, but did it really? Should it? And what of the magnificent demonstrations of courage, loyalty, compassion we see daily—have these found places in the pattern of thought with which we make our estimate of life? With which we act? Have we looked our speck of distance into the galaxy-strewn spaces and found nothing? Something? Or haven't we looked at all? Have we considered the worm on the leaf as sharing our condition? Have the very tools we use and the chores we do made their contributions? The Bible is full of religious language drawn from all the old trades and occupations of the world, from farming to the merchandising of fine jewels, and this suggests to me a wonderful relevance to life in all vital religion. I am afraid I cannot suggest offhand how to profit religiously from the battles of the detergents, mouthwashes and painkillers of our day, but I am sure these are all relevant. The question I am posing for our answering is simply, "Is the stuff of your life in your thought?"

There's a certain earthiness in vital religion, and the focal point of this earthiness is one's own existence—life and soul—and what we aim to do with it. I am *my* point of greatest awareness of the eternal mystery. What reveals nothing of me will reveal nothing of the other nor of God. Religion without the adventure of becoming is a poor business. The Calvinists subjected themselves to the severest discipline, however we may regard that discipline today. They took themselves seriously. So did Brother Lawrence, who practiced the presence of God. In some Mongol states the young male goes to do his stint in a monastery as our young men do in the army. Somehow or other one in possession of his or her soul displays interest in his or her own worth in some terms or other. Preoccupation with one's "sins" and unworthiness may be sickness, but no one ever acquired a healthy sense of being without making an honest estimate of oneself and endeavoring to overcome one's limitations. Not long ago an old man and philosopher, Martin Buber, challenged the state of Israel, his own state, on the question of the anticipated extermination of the Nazi war criminal Eichmann, and the world hardly noticed it. There could scarcely have been anything more beautifully in the tradition of the prophets of Israel, more reminiscent of Isaiah. What struck me about the incident was the feeling or awareness of the man's greatness in my own response. And why should I so feel? I believe it is because I saw here a man insisting *on being* in terms of what *ought to be*. Gandhi's sturdiness of spirit and emaciated body gave me the same feeling. Great acts are being as well as instances or doing.

This line of thought may lead some to remember preaching that asks us "to be good." I find it difficult to think in terms of "being good," so at times I use the concepts of beauty and of fulfillment, both borrowed, in preference to righteousness. I am shying away from the downgrading implicit in the old categories. Without adequate words I am trying to say that one should not feel downgraded by the discovery of his or her imperfections. One needs all one's resources for taking life seriously, which, by the way, is not a sissified preoccupation but the unparalleled adventure of human spirit.

But when it's all said and done, when I have thought and thought, and brought forth my bit of uncertain truth, was it worth the effort? In an eternity of darkness I have at best lighted a candle for myself that may be puffed out at any minute. My philosophy is but the flash of the firefly in a June meadow. The old problems and mysteries remain. Obviously I could remind myself that the flash of the firefly serves a useful purpose, but I wish to dig a bit deeper than that. I have had some happy associations with local church people recently, and especially in their effort to help each other confront the task of knowing about and building upon the patterns of thought and feeling by which they live. On my request many of them made statements, some of which are stirring and inspiring as well as thoughtful. One very young person wrote something which I used as a reading at a church service and was asked for by a university professor who was stirred by it. Like a statement I might make myself, these papers probe some problems and leave others untouched. They are generally characterized by statements of the problematic, by questions raised, and mysteries sensed more than by conclusions and answers. Some of them leap from the problem of existence to affirm a faith— a leap over contradictions, illogic, and injustices of existence—to affirm something. Should anyone feel this to be bad thinking? Kierkegaard did it, too, and it is quite possible that it is good thinking. It certainly can be good theologizing. But what I am leading to is this: if we have been of the opinion that the function of theologizing is just to take a rational account of reality, we are a bit short of the truth. This is not what we do even at our best. The religionist doesn't just collect evidence as a scientist does on the job. If that were so we should leave theology to these popes of the laboratory and let them tell us what to believe. But even if they found the truth they could not believe it for us. There is more involved—the dimensions of our needs, and the other agencies our spirits use. My appreciation and use of poetic imagination and my love of music and many things represent and serve needs as real as my rational needs, and they have nothing to do with science although science can serve them. We not only have to learn the truth, but to make our peace with it, and let no one despise that effort. Moreover, my truth may of necessity not be yours. Many truths are harsh. In the midst of our delights the writing on the wall appears. Moreover, we have to operate whether or not we have adequate knowledge, and the truth is that we shall never have adequate knowledge. Furthermore, we have to select from life's phenomena to get warmth for the heart as well as to get exercise and challenge for the brain cells. And when one has done his best, and even when that best is admirable, there are still the great problems and the mystery that will not be dispelled by any means. The realistic confrontation of the great and unyielding problem and mystery can be and often is a highly religious experience. In this conviction I have been confirmed by evidence in statements of belief that have been submitted to me. Take this brief one, for instance:

The only truly meaningful forces are hopeless riddles that most of us prefer to ignore as long as possible. Ultimately they must be faced. Preparation for dealing with an undefined but overwhelming force is terribly difficult, and yet we must live with the problem. The only answer is tentative and cautious at best. It demands an open mind, and an awareness of the human dilemma. It challenges us to constantly re-evaluate our relationships to all things—and most of all it implores us to never forget.

This young writer could not be accused of wanting to dodge reality. Yet can anyone have a moment's doubt as to the religiousness of this address to life?

The problematic and the mysterious are at the heart of religion and when they are once confronted without fear the most important part of the task is done. The cults presented us with mysteries—how the wine and bread became the body and blood of Christ, how the cross effected salvation, how Jesus could be both human and God, etc., and we were asked to take the doctrines on faith. So often our answers create mysteries as great as those they seek to dispel, and if we cannot find religiousness in the real mysteries I can hardly see how we can find it in facts or good reasoning either. As Robert Frost says of people in "The Cabin in the Clearing,"

> They will ask anyone there is to ask—
> In the fond faith accumulated fact
> Will of itself take fire and light the world up.

92

But darkness remains. Yet it can lose its terror for us. The individual can survive the open-eyed confrontation of reality, and there are times when people and cultures have to quit faking and look again into the face of God. This is necessary so that one may start again with fewer illusions, or at least with newer and more appropriate ones, and prepare the way for the fresh nativity of human hope and aspiration.

CHAPTER 12

An Honest Backward Look

Many of the local liberal church units are made up of escapees from mental confinement, spiritual refugees thrust upon their own resources, liberals who scarcely know how they happened, some who don't know the difference between a stubborn leftist theological position and liberal theology, and those born in the faith, some of whom were never "born again" in an experience of growth. So I think that it might profit us to have a look back to get more acquainted with some of the neglected realities of our situation; whence we've come and what we brought with us.

I have been lost in the deep woods more than once, and I learned rather early that to be sure I did not go around in circles I had to guide myself, not only by aiming at snags and trees ahead, but by keeping those I had passed in line, too.

A staggering percentage of us moved out of some other group into freedom, and this coming out requires some study. Robert Frost says:

> "The only certain freedom's in departure . . ."
> "The problem for the king is just how strict
> The lack of liberty, the squeeze of law
> And discipline should be in school and state
> To ensure a jet departure of our going
> Like a pip shot from 'twixt our pinching fingers."[1]

Let me never be caught telling what a modern poet really means. But I need not hesitate to say what meanings his words stir in me. In these words I find the joy of breaking away. And what departures we have known as a people! In the old days a youth could run away to sea. What a glorious moment when a young man mustered up the courage to roll the minimum necessities in his spare shirt and take off! So it must have been with many of us come-outers. We'll probably never again experience such release. The boy who went to sea soon bound himself to a captain who was ten times more restraining than his father, and so he might jump ship at the next port. Sooner or later, however, he had to learn to choose his strictures and coercions or be a roving, "no 'count" ship jumper all his days. Some leave their parent churches and, like the children of Israel, spend the next forty years in the wilderness somewhere between the Egyptians and the promised land. They are never going to be confined again, they think, until they find themselves in the toils of confinements not of their own choosing. I suspect the hermit crab must enjoy its naked release from its confining shell, but it had better make the road to the more commodious one as short as possible. What I am trying to say is that it is pretty futile to try to hang on to the moment of departure, for no one lives responsibly and uninvolved, too. The least the come-outer can do is to choose the confinements and dictates of freedom itself, and these are many and commanding too. Freedom has to be served, not plucked and consumed like an apple. We are often so conscious of departure that we are liable to be far more aware of our negations than our affirmations, and to avoid giving ourselves to anything.

I contend, too, that when we left we carried away more than we suspect. I have thought a great deal about my own background. I am one of those unfortunates who reads himself more than he does books, and along with the reading of books, and so I have to write in personal terms. There is a certain defense for so doing. If one is honest and unashamed of what he or she is or was, does not feel in the least superior to anyone, nor inferior either, and is really not afraid of either God or the devil, though a bit fond of both, one can afford to be personal. But let's make believe that I am not talking of myself.

Let me tell you part of the story of a come-outer. He came from a backwash of civilization, and was the first of his tribe ever to reach college. When he went home from school as a freshman he professed disbelief in the divinity of Jesus. Such apostasy had never before been voiced in his home community. He was subjected to a few

96

questions quietly and gently. Not one in his large family, including his parents, ever registered shock or disapproval, or voiced the feeling he had done wrong or had been disappointing. This was a family trait, an extremely important one for him. But there were additional factors that came from his Presbyterian faith that made a great difference in his life.

First, his faith took life very seriously. How one thought and felt and behaved made a great deal of difference, in cosmic as well as in personal terms. The all-seeing eye of God could not easily be put off the scent of the sinner. So, no matter how rebellious our young friend became he could never cease to be religious. Were he destined to be agnostic he was also destined to be devotedly and religiously so. If he became an atheist he would be reverently and devotedly atheistic. The Presbyterian cosmos was interested in him, and even though he lost his faith he could never lose a passionate interest in the cosmos as one involved in it. So no blossom could break the sod in spring without stirring mind and heart to dialogue and devotion. Life could not be trifled with, and it was compellingly interesting. Life demanded respect, and it was insistent in its demand to be understood. Life's joys could be heartily shared but in the knowledge that life could hurt deeply, that it summoned to great enterprise, and that man's response made all the difference.

The faith also spoke of God the good and the devil of evil at eternal war with each other. Both might be discredited (as they were), but the sense of right and wrong remained, along with the ever urgent need to differentiate between the true and the false, between the pretense and the reality of motive, between the genuine and the counterfeit.

In his home and church Jesus Christ was the centerpiece, and he had been fingered for the ministry when an infant. So he came to know Jesus better than most. He learned in time that he was a man, a great teacher, but not a God; that the miracles could not be rationally approved as historic; that he never rose from the dead; that many of the narratives of the New Testament were apocryphal, spurious, or mythical. Yet he read this man's teaching with an expectation very rare. The Bible, he found, was not identical with the word of God, but he never lost the feeling that the word was somewhere around and must be identified and more accurately stated and taken to heart.

And then there happened that which often happens between one and his or her God, something which a culture could not prevent while yet causing it. He responded to some of the teachings as he did not to others, and took some most seriously that the Christian church had not very often taken seriously. The little statements had the unusual punch. "Judge not," "Neither do I condemn you," "Love your enemies," "Behold the lilies of the field." So he learned that he should not condemn the sinner, that he should find a way to love the enemy, that he should never stoop to vengefulness. He read the simple words, "Let your yae be yae and your nae nae," and he could never get rid of their burning relevance to all he was or said or did. So he said what he thought. He became a bit of a pacifist, though a somewhat belligerent one. He came to think that God was an integral part of life, not a distant monarch. He thought divinity spoke in men's experiences before it could be heard from a book or a bush.

Presbyterian scholars introduced him to scientific thinking about the Bible. Teachers of physics and chemistry made him memorize the results of scientific work, but it took theologians to disclose something of the thought processes involved. He had Methodist teachers who brought him a strange but infectious concern for men and women on earth, for society. And he had Congregational teachers who introduced him to the historic protest against ecclesiasticism and the virtues of congregational autonomy. All of these teachings, so important to liberals, came to him before he ever heard of Universalists and Unitarians. In this state of mind he was graduated with special honors and then made to face a presbytery to be examined. Thus he learned that he had become an embarrassing problem to the brethren. I'll pass over the two-day conflict and heresy hunt that followed. At the end of the quizzing he asked why he had not been asked about his purpose in applying for the ministry. He was given five minutes, and he said in effect:

I believe in an indwelling spirit of life in man and in all life forms that I call God. I believe man is capable of redemption in this world and that human society is redeemable from war and savagery. I believe we should love our neighbors as ourselves, and seek for ways to love our enemies. I believe that I should try to remove every obstacle to the just treatment of all humans in society. I cannot bear false witness against anyone. I cannot betray a friend. I must speak as I think and feel. I believe in humanity and cannot be wholly a nationalist. I believe the creator gave me a mind to use, and so I cannot be altogether credulous about books and creeds. If my church cannot accept and use this kind of faith, I have been deceived and I would not touch its ministry with a ten-foot pole.

Then the gavel whanged and the chairman said, "Time's up." So Junior was turned out to the floor of the presbytery by this last and third committee and declared "unapproved." There followed a protest from several young ministers who said that if this young man could not be accepted they would have to resign their ministeries. So this body of conscientious men approved him, knowing they were disobeying orders, and formally laid themselves open to the censure of the General Assembly. Thus it was that the last service this denomination did for him was this act of honesty. Let no one suppose that there were no liabilities from his heritage—confining ideas, conflict, stupid men in authority, etc.—there were many. We don't need to remind each other of these. But we often do need to be reminded of some other things.

First, this young man's faith provided him with his basic value structure, and with values that helped make this structure operative. So if today he cannot snitch your property, this is why. If he cannot equivocate and evade, this is why. If he doesn't commit adultery or play the horses or borrow what he cannot hope to repay, or is in no danger of knocking your block off no matter how much he feels like it, this is why. If his word is as good as his bond, this is why. If he is one of those you would not need to fear even if there wasn't a law or police in the land, this is why. If he doesn't lay up treasures for the moth or the rust, this is why. If he persists in dreams of good things for humanity, this is why.

And there is something else which is of the greatest importance. Rabbi Klausner says of Jesus that his teachings were entirely from the Hebrew tradition, which is true, but that because of what he had accepted and rejected of that tradition, he became a cultural deviant, unacceptable to his own religious group. This is true of all the great religious leaders. So, too, was it true of this young man I have discussed. You don't have to be great to be a deviant. He was made what he was by the impact of a changing culture on his individual nature. It was because of some teachings he accepted from his tradition, as much as of those he rejected, that he became a rebel.

It should be said here, that this selecting and rejecting until one is at war with one's culture can work negatively, too, so that the worst aspects of a culture are cultivated as they were in Hitler and others. There is, for example, enough in the American culture to occasion a revolt either to the right or left if circumstances provide the stimulus.

So I suspect that, as I have said, we came out of orthodoxy, at least in part, in protest because of valuable contributions from that orthodoxy. I think it important to make this point because I believe that to be really and constructively free one has to make one's peace with one's cultural background, be it good or bad—a peace made up of some appreciation, some understanding, some forgiveness. We do this in retrospect for our parents when we outgrow adolescent rebellion, and we must do so with our cradle cultures. Let me quote Frost again. He says he is always a "pursuitist, never an escapist." I cannot think of any two words that put the issue so neatly. When we get over our sense of hurt and anger we can be pursuitists and leave off being escapists. Some are so shy of religion and church you can surmise they are trying to keep the first rapturous feeling of departure alive, and so can't give themselves to the command of any faith or cause. Here Frost again has something for us. "Don't be an agnostic," he advises. "Be something."

So if we have found a faith that commands us, some of us at least can say "thanks" to the folks who knocked us around a bit and loved us too, probably, but whose spiritual home could not be ours.

I'd like to come at the matter from another angle. The young man mentioned claimed his heritage gave him a value structure, and if this is so it did the same for those he left behind. I think of the importance of this fact in a democratic society. It seems generally understood that in a free society there must be a lot of people who are, largely, morally self-controlled and self-directed. In a free society we don't have to have the police breathing down our necks, and it must ever be thus in a free society. One of the Biblical prophets dreams of a time to come when the law will be written on the hearts of people, so that they will not need external direction, or to be told what to do. This is realized in a degree in a free society. And if democracy is to persist with a minimum of law, it has to have this ground of people who are as good or better than the state requires them to be. I think that our safety depends more on human decency than on law. There's truth in the old saying that we put locks on our doors to keep the honest people out. It is my conviction that if we lose enough of this moral self-direction in people, the police state is inevitable. I think this is the central issue facing democracy and not any of a number of things that are supposed to be crucial factors. I don't think, for example, that centralization versus wide distribution of government is the issue. (We can have tyranny on a half-acre as well as on a continent.)

The pertinence of all this to the subject will be evident, I hope, when we are reminded that we can find as big a percentage of honest Presbyterians, or Methodists, or Orthodox Jews, or Seventh-Day Adventists, or Jehovah's Witnesses or Holy Rollers sharing the

100

Jewish-Christian heritage as we can find of Unitarians or Universalists. It takes them all to hold the fort against tyranny. The percentages of denominations represented in *Who's Who* is not as important as this fact. If it were not for this body of people who claim and exercise the right of moral self-direction and of moral judgment, even upon the state, our theological protest would not be so securely tolerated, despite the contempt of orthodoxy for what we believe. They, the orthodox, are better for us than we know and we for them than they know. The Pilgrims were not Unitarians, nor listed in *Who's Who*, so how did they make the contribution they did make? Because they could do and be the truth they knew, and could not be mere obeyers of other people's laws. It makes me sick to witness the willingness today of orthodox Christians, and sometimes Jews, to have the state supervise the teaching of religion and even compose prayers their children mouth. This is the handwriting on the wall for modern orthodoxy. How easily history is forgotten!

Something else occurs to me. I have buried many people who for many years never darkened the doors of a church or synagogue. They were upright, often socially minded, gracious, lovely people, and courageous citizens. Yet, I observe that they lived on and by and under the command of the Jewish or Jewish-Christian ethic. They had walked out and said, probably for good reason, "a plague on all your churches," but they lived and breathed the code of decency which they did not and could not dump when they walked out of the churches.

Now let us switch back again to the thought that through selection and rejection one steps out of one's parents' faith, and becomes a cultural deviant who demands a higher code of morals than church or state represents. It is in this way that advances in human society are made. New truths, new knowledge, make this easier, even necessary. If the liberal movement is to justify itself, it must identify itself with this social function. Christian theology and symbol are becoming less and less suitable to the modern temper and modern knowledge. Surely here is a challenge to the come-outers. We acknowledge a great moral heritage from the culture from which we've come, and surely it is now our task to help with the process of restating our values and of creating suitable symbols and concepts. But instead of attacking this problem, Unitarian Universalists are shy of theology or philosophy. This is, in fact, a point at which we should be making a major contribution, for our protest was on theological grounds. Just to forsake the old is not enough. The fact that new values are emerging, and some threatening ones, makes it necessary for us to be as morally conscious as those who wrote the Ten Commandments and the Sermon on the Mount and the like. Our responsibilities as come-outers are considerable. We have lived on and protested in the name of moral and personal values that we imbibed with our mothers' milk. This is what we have with which to build a new world, or to conserve what we value in the present.

We should be very conscious of the values we hold in common with others, for there are indications of a break-up in our cultural values. Parents have again and again expressed to me their fear lest teaching children the Jewish-Christian moral values—the Golden Rule, etc.—will weaken them for the competition society forces upon them. Such values unfit them for participation in the jungle life of our time. So the summing-up is: Have a thought for the forces that made us, and for the value structure in terms of which we can grow and can judge of what is happening to the world. Jimmy Hoffa's thinking represents something very real in our world that we can never contend with alone. At the same time let's thank God for the departures we've made.

CHAPTER 13

The Wind in Both Ears

My father sent me up from the root cellar to see about the wind. He was rechecking the winter's potatoes to remove all signs of rot and was planning on setting out nets for some fresh cod later on. Was there a steady breeze, he wanted to know. Yes, there was. "Now face it," he said, "so that the wind sings in both your ears. Then tell me where your nose points to."

I cannot better describe what has been attempted in these pages. It has nothing to do with pessimism or optimism. We have no business with either. Optimism is not faith, and pessimism is worse than faithlessness. The whole book is a kind of wondering, and in this respect it is very like what we together seem to do. We wonder about truth, about all the whats and whys and whithers of life. Wondering is very important, but it should bear the fruits of faith and thought, and it should turn our faces to whatever is coming down the winds of time and circumstance. We should be finding ourselves on the highway to the realization of great human goals, but there is no clear light on the highway except as an individual may see it for himself. We have moved out of the theological underbrush into the open, and, though perhaps a bit dazzled by the light, should be moving swiftly and purposefully. But the light does not altogether fall on old and familiar things. The landscape and the shapes in the shadows of the future are strange, and maybe a bit unnerving. After all we did leave a protective covering in which humanity had been nurtured since the beginning. What is it that's coming down the wind to meet us? We have decided to make do with an orientation in this life, and all that lies between us and life's exits calls for courage, thought, and imagination, and active concern—as much as Heaven did and does for those we left behind. Light can be just as deceptive as darkness. The horizons shimmer, making visions uncertain. Things appear that aren't there at all. So much of what is there is strange and unknown. Our world has been immersed in man-made problems and threats, and these remain. And there is so much for which man is inadvertently responsible. Many good things, and many bad. We cannot be happy any longer with the thought that we did leave the bush.

Not long ago I visited a school which was under exceptionally good leadership. A teacher showed me around a shop in which children were working. We stopped to chat with Joey, who was aimlessly hammering on some metal. The teacher said, "Joey here is destined to be a consumer." When I smiled, the teacher looked at me sharply and said, "And don't belittle that role in the kind of society that we are building." I think we can guess at what he meant, but the remark set me to thinking of the portentous confluence of the population explosion and automation. Is it possible that not only the Joey's with defective intelligence will serve as mere consumers, but many with normal potential? Thousands of jobs are daily ceasing to be. As jobs go, will redeeming work go too? How shall self-respect be served? Where shall the many find great purposing? And the people immediately affected have little or no contact with us. We are largely segregated socially. The one unhappiness I have suffered in the company of "the saved" is that I miss those amongst whom I was reared, the educationally and economically unfortunate. They are people who have fought real battles in behalf of freedom. They are just as restless as anyone under domination, and just as responsive to freeing opportunity, and have less to lose than most of us in pursuing it. I can still find fellowship with them and do, but most of our people do not. We and they seem shy of each other. The barrier between us may be largely a matter of language, but if so, what a challenge language ought to be! Anyway, what is happening to them will change the face of the earth and all human relations; indeed, it has already. We have nothing to say about the greatest changes. We do not discuss them as matters waiting upon our decisions and votes. They happen. But need so much happen unmodified and undirected by human good will and intelligence? We live in an oasis of prosperity, and I for one have no great faith in its permanence and cannot have until good will and intelligence do some better teamwork in behalf of the unborn. Even should prosperity be maintained, we have long since learned that with it the individual can find life bitter and disappointing, and that we can deteriorate in affluence. We know that science, which unlocked the gates to affluence, is consequently not enough. Russell Davenport calls it "one-eyed and color blind" in its obsession with the quantitative and its neglect of the qualitative. And by the way, his book *The Dignity of Man* is half-read on my desk. In *My Country*, the author wrestles in a magnificent tussle with the angel of God.

> The vision that the world is waiting is
> The same that traced its way in wagon tracks
> Across empurpled plain and precipice,
> And whispered in the starlit tamaracks
> Where travellers told of freedom in the west
> Around the fires of hopeful bivouacs:
> The vision of a mighty purpose, presssed
> By all the peoples of the earth, to make
> The hidden truth within them manifest:
> And as this continent was free to take,
> And thus awoke the hope of all mankind,
> So now, in hope, we hear the future break
> On the unsovereigned beaches of the mind.[1]

Progress may be our most important product, but outside the context of hope and great purpose it is dynamite in a child's hands. Maybe this suggests in small measure why I feel, as I am sure others do, that we have need to understand ourselves better. I wouldn't have the chance of the proverbial snowball to improve myself without self-understanding, including awareness of my own limitations, and I cannot see that it is different with a religious fellowship.

We should understand our message. Many among us believe that we cannot have one as a group, and I have already indicated this. As I find Unitarian Universalists today, each of us may very well feel that he or she understands what we stand for in common, but that no one agrees with any one individual's perception of what it is. The statement is admittedly an exaggeration, but not much of one. This state of affairs may be harmless within a framework of assumed values such as the will to peace and human unity, the right to think for oneself, and the right of all people to political and religious liberty, and to the physical necessities in a world of plenty. If we have such operating values, as I believe we do, we do have a faith. But many among us do not acknowledge common values, and many, too, actually believe little or nothing that will direct and discipline them. A faith, nevertheless, we must have, and it must somehow become articulate.

> Let us not fear Man: let us fear
> Only what he believes in . . .
> It is Nothing that we must fear: the thought of Nothing:
> The sound of Nothing in our hearts . . .
> The belief in nothing.[2]

Without such values as mentioned above there would be no ethical or theological sense at all to our existence as a group. With them, and with the rapid growth of knowledge of humanity and the universe there are untold riches for the mind, stuff for the formulation of a faith. We should be lost in explaining our faith to new members without the written efforts of individual ministers and laypeople, and those of some outsiders too. Some of these statements differ widely, but they are rich in resources for a survey of what we believe and value in common. And why not such a survey? Would it bind us? Not if it were done periodically and were taken as no more than a survey. Isn't it possible that in our fear of creeds we are walking backwards and forgetting that great liberating documents such as the Bill of Rights have been written and have remained with us as bulwarks of freedom? Is religion by nature incapable of producing a freeing document? We have had individual statements and factional manifestoes, but we need more than these. Need a free fellowship be speechless in its own defense? The recent appointment of commissions to study our faith is most promising. They will be most useful providing their products contain authentic pictures of what we are as well as the members' notions of what we ought to believe and do. I believe that the survey should have been their first assignment, to serve us as a mirror in which to see ourselves.

Some things I have already discussed, but the urgency of my feelings forces me to mention them again. A better understanding, for instance, of the concept most frequently on our tongues, that of freedom. There seems to be a confusion of freedom and individualism. Individualism has its own value, but it is not the same thing as the social concept of freedom, which could only arise as a way of relating to people, all people. One's experience alone in the wilderness can be highly cherishable, but it has no relation to freedom in the sense we use the term. Freedom is a way of relating, not just independence, however valuable independence may be. Indepen-

106

dence can be, and often is, among us, socially irresponsible or the badge of special privilege. But as liberal religionists, we should be deeply committed to the full sharing of whatever privilege we seek and enjoy for ourselves. Many of us experienced a warmth of heart in knowing that so many Unitarian Universalists, including our president, walked in the now famous march on Washington. It was more than a gesture, something deeply revealing and reassuring. This brings to mind another problem with which we have been grappling for some time. Church people used to enjoy a fellowship in good works because good works were centered in the churches. Now in the day of agencies it is quite different, and for some reason in many churches no one knows what the other fellow is doing, if anything. The great loss is not knowing what is being done. The situation is worsened by the feeling often expressed that good works and the promotion of good causes are a private and personal matter. There is also often a strong objection to what is called a "social creed" or anything in the way of ethical commitment of a church of denomination. No single person or group, it is contended, can represent the church, local or national, despite the fact that the church cannot escape having some kind of community significance. A church that is not concerned with the ills of the world except through the pulpit has that kind of significance at least. As I said before, any percentage below a hundred, it is often claimed, has no representational rights. This is a formidable handicap. But it is so often met with in our midst that we must make the best of every other approach and hope for a break-through sometime. But before we go into that, why are we this way? Have our notions of freedom and of democratic operation anything to do with it? Are those notions valid? What has what is known about effective education to say about it? We still love to think that it is enough to discharge arrows of good will and truth on Sunday morning in the fond hope that later we shall find them in the hearts of the converted. It happens all right. Just yesterday a member of the Yankee baseball team told a television audience of how he struck a foul ball into the stands that contained over sixty-five thousand people and hit his mother with it. This is an illustration in reverse, but it does show that the random shot may find its target. But nevertheless we need, as we always have, the fellowship of good works and active support of causes. Suppose we grant the minority its claim, "You can't do anything as a church because if you do you'll misrepresent me." A suggestion has been made, one that some local units already use, that our church offices have a record of what our members and adherents (to use a Presbyterian phrase) actually do. There is even objection to this. Some feel about good works as Jesus felt about praying. They should be done in secret. But I have pointed out the loss this involves. To a new minister in a church, or to the minister of a large church, it would be most helpful in directing new members who wish to be involved in something they feel is of great worth. It would help us know what we really are doing, and might help ministers avoid scolding some people for not doing something they've been busy at for years. There are always ways of serving the individual adequately without the loss of all sense of a community of faith, or of institutional significance, and we have come too close to losing both. Anyone who does not cotton to this suggestion is still faced with the responsibility of doing something with the problem. The worst that can happen to us is to hush it all up because it is difficult.

With our noses to the winds of the future we may also discover a need to find a fresh orientation to history relevant to our sensitivities and values. Some of us must feel at times like the cartoon character who walks off a cliff onto the unsubstantial air and then falls when it becomes aware of its situation. So maybe we shouldn't raise the question. But while we make any claim to self-awareness, or even to intelligence in religion, we must raise it.

Who can have a sense of direction without an historic sense? Who without a strong historic sense can affect the course of history? History's tragic mistakes can be made again. We differ in our present attitudes too widely. Some people would have nothing but a Christian heritage, despite the fact that Christianity repudiates, and always has repudiated, many of the things they stand for. Some don't give a fig for the past, and walk in innocent vulnerability, waiting for the future to overwhelm them. Many of us have, by adoption, added the wisdom of world religions and human experience generally to our Christian heritage, and I personally feel that this we must do if we are to contribute to human destiny. But the question is wide open and not yet answered in any way that can grip and serve our people.

As I have pointed out, we share a goodly heritage with Christian faiths and other faiths in the matter of ethical values, despite the fact that we have had such a theological housecleaning. We are more unique and significant for our housecleaning than for our new furnishings. Since we branched off from Protestantism we think too negatively of our heritage. Luther suggested the doctrine of the priesthood of all believers, but, from our standpoint, for the wrong reason. He did not protest corruption as much as what he regarded as the wrong doctrine of salvation. He had no faith in humankind or society. Neither did Zwingli, whose military authoritarianism cancelled out any great value he may have had. Calvin was interested in society and brought a cruel, bloody theocracy to bear upon it. But the era of the Reformation did have those who spoke our language, spoke of the free soul, of reason in religion, and the possibility of garnering the wisdom of all great faiths, and the like. There were those, too, who just wished to be left alone. We owe more to the Anabaptists in their fight for religious liberty than we do to the great movements that emerged from the Reformation. In Ohio, where I live, we often meet broad-hatted and bewhiskered men in buggies on the highway. We are inclined to pity them, but perhaps we should, in a manner of speaking, remove our hats, cross ourselves, and remember how they were driven to the frontiers of society to endure; and also to remember that there are no such frontiers now left, and that what states failed to do to them, the climate of a culture they cannot escape will do eventually.

We are particularly indebted to such individuals as Erasmus who sought no break with church or society, but wanted only the right to think and interpret the various faiths for themselves, "the disciples of the free spirit" as some call them. Many of them remained and were absorbed in time, while no doubt leavening the faiths of Europe. Others were expelled and rejected and wandered about, some of them, like Servetus, later caught and destroyed. Some were compelled by this rejection to form groups, the Socinians and the much later Universalists. The Universalists always have had a yen towards remaining in the old groups as a leavening force. In America they had to form a church and to fight one of America's greatest battles. They won it and then began at once to disintegrate, and were saved again by the general rejection of their increasing rationalism and their increasing tendency to give weight to the doctrine of God's immanence.

Roland Bainton says, "The rationalists' aversion to theological niceties could be undergirded by the mystics' indifference to credal refinements. . . . The disciples of the free spirit, if they may be so designated, did very little by way of forming new churches, partly because they could spiritualize the teachings and rites of any church, and preferred to remain where they felt at home unless expelled. If cast out they were too indifferent to set about the erection of new organizations."[3]

We inherited something of this weakness, and I must call it a weakness in our time when corporate evil must be met by corporate as well as personal good. In addition, many of the hurt and angry souls of our time have joined and are joining us, in such a state of negation that they are highly suspicious of any forms, or of any common profession of faith, or any discipline, or even of any religious tradition—and, believe it or not, suspicious too of any religious speculation. They stay together because of a shared protest and a sense of individual independence. Thus we face the problem of creating a strong free church.

There is also a theological threat to our unity. I don't mean for a minute that differences of belief or complete freedom within a working and constantly transformed value structure, is a threat. The threat is in group weakness. Bainton says, in effect, in the book just referred to, that the mystics had a direct contact with deity that could bypass the authorities, and thus nullify the idea of salvation through one great historic event. We still have mystics of a sort who, I believe, retain the great values of mysticism. They do not often seek personal union with God, but they experience something akin to it in non-theistic terms in their direct approach to reality. But a point that needs to be made is that rationalism serves the same purpose, giving men and women the means to effect their own salvation. Partly for such reasons, neither the mystic nor the rationalist contributes greatly to the strength of a church, any more than to a theology, if history tells the truth. So the question is, is increased church strength possible while freedom endures? On the other hand, will a faith unsupported by organizational strength be absorbed by the orthodoxies of suburbia if by nothing else? No easy answer either way should be given, but it seems that in our time when there is no possible flight to freedom, freedom has to develop an organic strength that will be more support than threat to it. Anyway, let's keep the wind singing in both ears, and pray for the courage to interpret and act upon what it brings to us.

Notes

Chapter 2

1. Emily Dickinson, *The Poems of Emily Dickinson,* ed. Thomas H. Johnson (Cambridge, Mass.: The Belknap Press of Harvard University Press, 1951), No. 1129.

Chapter 3

1. William James, *The Varieties of Religious Experience* (New York: New American Library, A Mentor Book, 1958).
2. *Ibid.*, p. 130.
3. Gordon Allport, *The Individual and His Religion* (New York: The Macmillan Company, 1957), Ch. 3.

Chapter 5

1. Viktor Frankl, *Mans' Search for Meaning: An Introduction to Logotherapy* (Boston: Beacon Press, 1962).
2. Eric Fromm, *Psychoanalysis and Religion* (New Haven: Yale University Press, 1950).
3. Robert Frost, "On a Tree Fallen Across the Road," *Complete Poems of Robert Frost* (New York: Holt, Rinehart and Winston, Inc., 1949), p. 296.
4. II Timothy 1:7.

Chapter 6

1. Carl Jung, *Modern Man in Search of a Soul* (New York: Harcourt, Brace & World, Harvest Books), pp. 235–236.

Chapter 7

1. W. H. Auden, "In Time of War," *The Collected Poetry of W. H. Auden* (New York, Random House).
2. Charles Frankel, *The Case for Modern Man* (Boston: Beacon Press, paperback, 1959), p. 207.
3. *Ibid.*, p. 202.

Chapter 8

1. *Life* magazine, January 5, 1962.

Chapter 9

1. Carl Jung, *The Undiscovered Self* (Boston: Little, Brown, and Company, 1957).
2. *See* Jacob Trapp, "The Inward Way," *Minns Lectures. See also* Arthur Foote, D.D., "The Meaning of Depth Psychology for Liberal Religion," *Minns Lectures,* Fall 1959. Published by The Trustees of the Minns Lectureship.

Chapter 10

1. Archibald MacLeish, *J. B.* (Boston: Houghton Mifflin Co. 1958), p. 13.
2. Paul Tillich, "What Is Truth?" *The New Being* (New York: Charles Scribner's Sons, 1955), Ch. 8, pp. 65–67.
3. Walter Kaufmann, *The Faith of a Heretic* (New York: Doubleday & Company).
4. Gerhard Szczesny, *The Future of Unbelief* (New York: George Braziller, Inc., 1961).

Chapter 11

1. Albert Camus, *Actuelles II.* Quoted by Thomas Hanna in *The Thought and Art of Albert Camus* (Chicago: Henry Regnery Company, 1959).

Chapter 12

1. Robert Frost, "How Hard It Is to Keep From Being King," *The Poetry of Robert Frost* (New York: Holt, Rinehart and Winston, Inc., 1962).

Chapter 13

1. Russell Davenport, *My Country, A Poem of America* (New York: Simon and Schuster, Inc., 1944), p. 54.
2. *Ibid.*, pp. 16, 18.
3. Roland Bainton, *The Reformation of the Sixteenth Century* (Boston: Beacon Press, 1952), p. 126.